Mosab Hassan Yousef

Biography

Journey of Faith and Betrayal

Scott Allen

CONTENT

Chapter 1: Captured

Chapter 2: The Faith Ladder

Chapter 3: Throwing Stones

Chapter 4: Survival

Chapter 5: A Hero's Return

Chapter 6: Radical

Chapter 7: Fanning the Flames

Chapter 8: Guns

Chapter 9: The Slaughterhouse

Chapter 10: The Offer

Chapter 11: Number 823

Chapter 12: Trust No One

Chapter 13: Riot

Chapter 14: Damascus Road

Chapter 15: Second Intifada

Chapter 16: Undercover

Chapter 17: Most Wanted

Chapter 18: Torn

Chapter 19: The Game

Chapter 20: Defensive Shield

Chapter 21: Supernatural Protection

Chapter 22: Protective Custody

Chapter 23: A Vision for Hamas

Chapter 24: Good-Bye

Chapter 1: Captured

I guided my little white Subaru around a blind turn on one of the narrow lanes leading to the main highway near Ramallah, West Bank. I approached one of the several checkpoints that dot the roads leading to and from Jerusalem, lightly stepping on the brake.

"Stop the engine!" Someone yelled in shaky Arabic, "Stop the car!" Six Israeli soldiers stepped out of the bushes and blocked my automobile, each carrying a machine gun and pointing it squarely at my head.

Panic rose to the surface of my throat. I came to a halt and flung the keys out the open window.

"Get the hell out!" "Get the hell out!"

Without missing a beat, one of the men yanked open the door and flung me to the dusty ground. I had hardly covered my head before the beating began. Even as I tried to shield my face, the soldiers' heavy boots rapidly found other targets: ribs, kidneys, back, neck, and skull.

Two of the men dragged me to my feet and to the checkpoint, where I was made to kneel behind a cement wall. My hands were tied behind my back with a sharp-edged plastic zip tie that was too tightly knotted. Someone blindfolded me and pushed me onto the floor of a jeep. Fear and resentment mixed as I worried where they were bringing me and how long I'd be gone. I was only eighteen years old and a few weeks away from finishing high school. What was going to become of me?

The jeep came to a halt after only a short distance. A soldier approached me from behind and removed my blindfold. I discovered we were at Ofer Army Base after squinting in the intense sunlight. Ofer, an Israeli defence base, was one of the West Bank's largest and most guarded military facilities.

We passed many armoured tanks that were veiled by canvas tarps as we went toward the main facility. The huge mounds had always piqued my interest whenever I saw them from outside the walls. They appeared to be massive, enormous boulders.

We were greeted by a doctor who gave me a short once-over, supposedly to ensure I was fit to withstand interrogation. I must have passed since the handcuffs and blindfold were replaced and I was forced back into the jeep within minutes.

One burly soldier put his boot squarely on my hip and slammed the barrel of his M16 assault rifle into my breast as I tried to bend my body to fit into the narrow area usually occupied for people's feet. The strong odour of gasoline permeated the vehicle's floor and squeezed my throat shut. The soldier shoved the rifle barrel deeper into my chest whenever I tried to modify my constricted posture.

A burning ache raced through my body, causing my toes to clench. It felt like a rocket exploded inside my head. The intensity of the impact had come from the front seat, and I recognized that one of the troops had hit me in the head with his rifle butt. He hit me again before I could defend myself, this time harder and in the eye. I tried to get away, but the soldier who had been using me as a footstool dragged me up.

"Don't move or I will shoot you!" he exclaimed.

But I couldn't help myself. Every time one of his comrades attacked me, I recoiled automatically.

My eye was starting to swell shut under the thick blindfold, and my face felt numb. My legs didn't have any circulation. My respiration came out in short, weak gasps. I'd never known such agony. The dread of being at the mercy of something ruthless, primal, and inhuman was worse than the physical anguish. My mind raced as I tried to decipher the motivations of my tormentors. Fighting and murdering could be motivated by hatred, fury, vengeance, or even need. But I hadn't done anything wrong to these soldiers. I hadn't fought back. I had completed all of the tasks assigned to me. I posed no danger to them. I was chained, blindfolded, and defenceless. What was it about these folks that made them like hurting me so much? Even the most heinous animal slaughters are done for a reason, not just for sport.

I imagined how my mother would react if she found out I had been detained. With my father already imprisoned in Israel, I was the man of the house. Would I be imprisoned for months or years, like he had been? If that's the case, how will my mother cope without me? I began to grasp how my father felt—concern for his family and grief at the fact that we were concerned about him. As I imagined my mother's face, tears welled up in my eyes.

I also questioned if all of my high school years were going to be for naught. If I were to be imprisoned in Israel, I would have to miss my final examinations next month. Even as the blows continued to land, my thoughts were filled with questions and cries: Why are you doing this to me? What did I do? No, I'm not a terrorist! I'm only a kid. Why are you beating me this way?

I believe I passed out numerous times, but every time I awoke, the troops were still striking me. I couldn't get away from the strikes. The only thing I could think of was to shout. I gagged and vomited all over myself as I felt bile rising in the back of my throat.

Before I passed out, I felt tremendous grief. Was this the conclusion of the story? Was I going to perish before my life had even begun?

Chapter 2: The Faith Ladder

Mosab Hassan Yousef is my name.

I am the eldest son of Sheikh Hassan Yousef, one of the Hamas organisation's seven founders. I was born in Ramallah, West Bank, and come from one of the most religious Islamic families in the Middle East.

My narrative begins with my grandpa, Sheikh Yousef Dawood, who was the religious leader—or imam—for the town of Al-Janiya, which is located in the region of Israel known as Judea and Samaria in the Bible. My grandfather was my hero. When he held me, his soft, white beard tickled my cheek, and I could sit for hours listening to the sound of his wonderful voice chanting the adhan—the Muslim call to prayer. And I had plenty of chances to do so because Muslims are required to pray five times every day. Chanting adhan and the Qur'an is difficult, but when my grandfather performed it, the music was amazing.

Some chanters used to upset me so badly as a kid that I wanted to stick rags in my ears. But my grandfather was a passionate man, and as he sang, he immersed his audience in the significance of the adhan. He trusted all he was told.

During Jordanian authority and Israeli occupation, Al-Janiya had a population of about 400 people. However, the citizens of this small rural community were uninterested in politics. Al-Janiya was a very serene and picturesque hamlet nestled amid the gently sloping hills a few kilometres northwest of Ramallah. Its sunsets painted everything in rose and violet hues. The air was clean and clear, and you could see all the way to the Mediterranean from many of the hills' peaks.

Every morning at four o'clock, my grandfather was on his way to the mosque. After finishing his morning prayers, he would ride his donkey to the field, cultivate the soil, maintain his olive trees, and drink fresh water from the mountain spring. There was no pollution in the air because only one individual in Al-Janiya owned an automobile.

My grandfather had a continuous stream of visitors when he was at home. He was more than just the imam to the residents of that village. He prayed over each newborn baby, whispering the adhan into the child's ear. When someone died, my grandfather cleansed, anointed, and wrapped the body in winding cloth. He married them and buried them both.

Hassan, my father, was his favourite son. My father went to the mosque with my grandfather even as a young lad, before it was required of him. None of his brothers were as interested in Islam as he was.

Hassan learned to chant the adhan at his father's side. And, like his father, he had a voice and a passion that drew people to him. My grandfather was ecstatic about him. My grandfather told my father when he was twelve years old, "Hassan, you have shown that you are very interested in God and Islam." So I'm sending you to Jerusalem to study Sharia." Sharia is Islamic religious law that governs aspects of daily life such as family and cleanliness, as well as politics and economy.

Hassan was uninterested in politics or economics. He only desired to emulate his father. He desired to read and chant the Qur'an as well as assist the community. But he was about to discover that his father was much more than a dependable religious leader and a well-liked public worker.

Because beliefs and traditions have always mattered more to the Arab people than government constitutions and courts, men like my grandpa frequently rose to positions of power. The word of a religious leader was regarded as law, especially in areas where secular leaders were weak or corrupt.

My father was not sent to Jerusalem to study religion; rather, his father was grooming him to govern. So, for the next few years, my father lived and studied in the Old City of Jerusalem, near the Dome of the Rock—the iconic golden-domed monument that most people across the world associate with Jerusalem. He finished his studies at the age of eighteen and proceeded to Ramallah, where he was hired as the imam of the Old Town mosque. My father, filled with a desire to serve both Allah and his people, was ready to begin his work in that town, as his father had done in Al-Janiya.

However, Ramallah was not Al-Janiya. The former was a thriving metropolis. The latter was a sleepy small town. My father was surprised to find only five old guys waiting for him when he initially entered the mosque.

Everyone else seemed to be drinking and gambling in coffeehouses and pornographic theatres. Even the man who sang the adhan for the mosque next door had run a microphone and cord from the minaret to keep the Islamic ritual going without interfering with his poker game.

My father's heart broke for these folks, but he wasn't sure how he'd ever get to them. Even his five old men stated that they had come to the mosque because they knew they were dying soon and wanted to go to heaven, but they were at least prepared to listen. As a result, he made do with what he had. He led these men in prayer and instructed them on the Qur'an. They began to love him as if he were an angel sent from heaven in a very short period of time.

It was a different story outside the mosque. Many others were angry because my father's passion for the god of the Qur'an showed their own casual approach to the faith.

People sneered as they pointed to my baby-faced father, asking, "Who is this child doing the adhan?" "He has no place here. He is a nuisance."

"Why is this little guy making us look bad?" Only the elderly visit the mosque."

"I would rather be a dog than be like you," one of them yelled in his face.

My father endured the persecution quietly, without retaliating or defending himself. But his compassion and love for the people would not allow him to give up. And he kept doing what he was called to do: pushing people to return to Islam and Allah.

He expressed his concerns to my grandfather, who quickly recognized that my father has much more fire and talent than he had previously imagined. My grandfather sent him to Jordan to further his Islamic studies. As you shall see, the people he met there changed the path of my family's history and even the history of conflict in the Middle East. But, before I go any further, I need to explain a few key elements in Islamic history that will help you understand why the innumerable diplomatic solutions that have been proposed have all failed and give no chance for peace.

Chapter 3: Throwing Stones

Hamas wanted a move—any move—that could be used to justify an uprising. Even though it was all a tragic mistake, the move took place in early December 1987.

The First Intifada had begun, and the Palestinian cause had made international headlines. Everything changed in our cemetery-playground when the intifada began. Every day, more people arrive than ever before. Anger and wrath stalked beside grief. Palestinian mobs began stone-throwing at Jews who had to drive past the cemetery to reach the Israeli settlement a mile distant. Israeli settlers with heavy weapons slaughtered at will. When the Israel Defense Forces (IDF) arrived, there was more shooting, more injured, and more killing.

Our house was bang in the middle of everything. Israeli bullets smashed the water storage tanks on our roof numerous times. The dead remains delivered to our graveyard by the masked fedayeen, or liberation warriors, were no longer only old folks. They were sometimes still-bleeding bodies on stretchers, unwashed and unwrapped in winding blankets. Each martyr was buried promptly so that no one could take the bodies, steal the organs, and return the stuffed corpses to their relatives.

There was so much violence that I felt bored a few times when everything was peaceful. My buddies and I began hurling stones as well, in order to stir things up and gain respect as resistance fighters. The Israeli settlement, high on top of the mountain, was visible from the cemetery, protected by a high fence and guard towers. I thought about the 500 individuals who lived there and drove new automobiles, many of which were armoured. They were armed with automatic rifles and appeared to be free to shoot anybody they pleased. They appeared to a ten-year-old child to be aliens from another planet.

Some friends and I hid beside the road one evening right before sunset prayer. We chose a settlers' bus as a target because it was larger than a car and would be simpler to strike. We knew the bus arrived at the same time every day. The familiar sounds of the imam repeated over the loudspeakers while we waited, and when we finally heard the faint rumble of a diesel engine, we each picked up two stones. We knew where the bus was even though we were hiding and couldn't see the roadway. We jumped up at precisely the perfect moment and let our ammunition fly. The distinct sound of stone striking metal convinced us that at least some of our projectiles had hit their mark.

It wasn't, however, the bus. It was a large military van packed with agitated Israeli soldiers. As the truck came to a stop, we hurriedly dived back into our ditch hiding spot. The soldiers couldn't see us, and we couldn't see them. So they simply began shooting into the air. They continued to fire aimlessly for a few minutes, and we hastily made our way into a nearby mosque, diving low.

Prayer had already begun, but I don't think anyone was paying attention to what they were saying. Everyone was wondering what was going on as they heard automatic rifles stuttering outside. My pals and I slid into the final row of the line, thinking no one would notice. However, once the imam ended his prayers, every hostile eye turned toward us.

IDF vehicles screeched to a halt in front of the mosque within seconds. Soldiers stormed into the room, pulling us all outside and ordering us to lie facedown on the ground while they checked our identification. I was the last one to go, fearful that the military would suspect me of causing all the trouble. I was certain they would beat me to death. But no one seemed to notice me. Perhaps they reasoned that a kid like me wouldn't have the audacity to throw pebbles at an IDF vehicle. Whatever the reason, I was relieved they weren't after me. The inquiry lasted several hours, and I knew that many of those present were upset with me. They might not have known exactly what I'd done, but there was no doubt that I'd set off the raid. I didn't mind. I was truly ecstatic. My buddies and I had stood up to the power of the Israeli army and emerged unscathed. The adrenaline was intoxicating, and it made us even more daring.

Another day, a friend and I hid again, this time closer to the road. When a settler automobile arrived, I stood up and flung a stone as hard as I could. It shattered the windshield, making the sound of a bomb bursting. It didn't break the glass, but I could see the driver's scared expression. He drove another forty yards or so before slamming on the brakes and shifting into reverse.

I dashed into a cemetery. He followed but stood outside, leaning against the wall and scanning the graveyard for me. My friend had bolted in the opposite direction, leaving me alone in the face of an enraged, armed Israeli settler.

I laid peacefully on the ground between the graves, knowing that the driver was only waiting for me to raise my head over the low gravestone. Finally, the stress became too much for me; I couldn't sit motionless any longer. I got to my feet and raced as fast as I could. Fortunately, it was getting dark, and he didn't seem to want to go into the cemetery.

I hadn't gone very far when my feet slipped out from under me. I found myself at the bottom of an open grave, waiting for the next person to die. Is that supposed to be me? I was perplexed. The Israeli blasted rounds into the graveyard above me. Stone shards poured down on the grave.

I knelt there, unable to move. I heard people chatting after about half an hour, so I knew he had gone and it was safe to get out.

A few days later, when I was strolling down the street, the identical automobile passed me. This time there were two males in it, but the driver was the same. He recognized me and swiftly exited the vehicle. I tried to run again, but this time I was unsuccessful. He grabbed my arm, slapped me across the face, and hauled me back to the car. As we approached the settlement, no one said anything. Both men appeared anxious and held their pistols, occasionally turning to stare at me in the backseat. I was a scared little kid, not a terrorist. They, on the other hand, acted like trophy tiger hunters.

A soldier checked the driver's ID and waved him past the barrier. Didn't he wonder why these guys were carrying a Palestinian child? I knew I should be afraid, and I was, but I couldn't help but look around. I'd never visited an Israeli settlement before. It was stunning. Clean streets, pools, and a breathtaking view of the valley from the mountaintop.

The driver drove me to an IDF base inside the settlement, where soldiers seized my shoes and forced me to sit on the ground. I assumed they were going to shoot me and bury my body somewhere in the countryside. They told me to go home when it started to grow dark.

My residence was nearly a mile away. I walked back in my socks, gritting my teeth as the rocks and gravel dug into my feet's soles. When my mother spotted me approaching, she raced down the walkway and held me tightly, nearly squeezing the air from my lungs. She had been told that I had been kidnapped by Israeli settlers and that they would kill me. She scolded me for being so stupid over and over again, all the while caressing my head and clutching me securely against her chest.

You'd think I'd learnt my lesson, but I was a stupid young kid. I couldn't wait to tell my cowardly pals about my brave exploits. By 1989, it was common for Israeli troops to knock on our door and force their way inside. They looked to be on the lookout for someone who had thrown stones and fled through our property. The soldiers were constantly highly armed, and I couldn't figure out why they were so concerned over a few rocks.

I felt a rush of admiration for my father as we settled in and began to eat. I could see the tiredness on his face, but I also knew how much he enjoyed his job. Only his dedication to Allah matched his grace for the individuals he served. I was thinking about how different he was from most Muslim males as I observed him converse with my mother and brothers and sisters. He never hesitated to assist my mother around the house or to look after us children. In fact, dad cleaned his own socks in the sink every night so my mother wouldn't have to. In a culture where women considered it an honour to scrub their husbands' legs after a long day, this was unheard of.

We had never spent the night before without our father. Even though he was usually busy, he was always home in the evenings. He was the one who woke us up every morning for dawn prayer and drove us to school. What if he doesn't return home tonight?

We went to the Red Cross the next day to see if we could find out anything about my father's absence. The man at the desk informed us that he had been arrested but that the IDF would not provide any information to the Red Cross for at least eighteen days.

We returned home to count down the two and a half weeks that had passed. We didn't hear anything for the entire time. I returned to the Red Cross when the eighteen days were up to see what they had learned. They assured me there was no fresh information.

We only found out later that he had been transferred to Maskobiyeh, an Israeli interrogation facility, where he had been tortured and questioned. The Shin Bet, Israel's internal security service, was aware that my father was at the highest level of Hamas and presumed that he was aware of everything that occurred or was planned. And they were determined to extract it from him.

He didn't tell me what really happened until many years later. He was handcuffed and hung from the ceiling for days. They shocked him with electricity till he passed out. They placed him with collaborators known as "birds," in the hopes that he would talk to them. When it didn't work, they beat him some more. But my father was a fighter. He kept quiet, never providing the Israelis any information that could be used against Hamas or his Palestinian brethren.

Chapter 4: Survival

The Israelis believed that if they seized one of Hamas' leaders, things would improve. But, while my father was in prison, the intifada became even more brutal. Amer Abu Sarhan of Ramallah had seen enough Palestinian fatalities by late 1989. He seized a kitchen knife and stabbed three Israelis to death, thereby starting a revolution. This incident marked the beginning of a considerable increase in violence.

Sarhan became a hero to Palestinians who had lost friends or family members, had their land confiscated, or had any other motive to seek vengeance. They were not by nature terrorists. They were simply people who had run out of alternatives and hope. Their backs were against the wall. They had nothing left to lose and nothing to gain. They didn't care about what the rest of the world thought or even about their own lives.

Going to school became a major issue for us youngsters back then. It was not uncommon for me to walk out of school to find Israeli jeeps driving up and down the streets, loudspeakers announcing an instant curfew. Curfews were taken very seriously by the Israeli military. These were not curfews in American cities, where officials would contact a teen's parents if he was spotted driving after 11 p.m. If a curfew was announced in Palestine and you were out on the street for any reason, you were shot. There was no warning and no arrest. You were recently shot.

I didn't know what to do the first time a curfew was called while I was at school. I had a four-mile trek ahead of me and knew I wouldn't make it home by curfew. I was afraid because the streets were already deserted. I couldn't stay where I was, and even though I was just a kid trying to get home from school, I knew the troops would shoot me if they saw me. Many Palestinian children were killed.

I started scurrying from house to house, creeping through backyards and hiding in bushes along the route. I did my best to dodge barking dogs and guys with machine guns, and when I finally turned the corner onto our street, I was relieved to find that my brothers and sisters had arrived safely.

However, curfews were only one of the changes brought about by the intifada. On numerous occasions, a masked man would appear at school and inform everyone that a strike had been declared and that they should go home. The strikes, called by one of the Palestinian groups, were intended to financially harm Israel by lowering sales tax revenue collected from business owners. The owners would have to pay less tax if the stores were closed. However, the Israelis were not foolish. They've only recently begun arresting shops for tax evasion. So, who suffered as a result of the strikes?

Furthermore, the numerous resistance organisations were always competing for power and prestige. They were like children squabbling over a soccer ball. Nonetheless, Hamas was rapidly gaining power and had begun to challenge the Palestine Liberation Organization's (PLO) dominance.

* * *

The Palestinian Liberation Organization (PLO) was founded in 1964 to represent the Palestinian people. Its three largest member organisations are Fatah, a left-wing nationalist group; the Popular Front for the Liberation of Palestine (PFLP), a communist group; and the Democratic Front for the Liberation of Palestine (DFLP), which is also communist in ideology.

The PLO asked that Israel return all land that had previously belonged to Palestinian regions and provide Palestine the right to self-determination. To that purpose, it waged a global public relations, guerilla warfare, and terrorism campaign from its base in neighbouring Jordan, then in Lebanon and Tunisia.

Unlike Hamas and Islamic Jihad, the PLO was never fundamentally Islamic. Its members were nationalists, not all of whom were practising Muslims. Many of them, in fact, did not believe in God. I regarded the PLO as crooked and self-serving even as a young lad. Its leaders dispatched individuals, many of whom were minors, to carry out one or two high-profile terrorist assaults per year in order to legitimise fund-raising for the anti-Israel battle. The teenage fedayeen were merely fuel to feed the fires of rage and hatred, and to keep the money going into the personal bank accounts of PLO leaders.

After a while, the turmoil and confusion became almost comical. When an exam was planned, my classmates and I convinced older students to attend school wearing masks and claiming there was a strike. We thought it was entertaining.

In short, we were turning against ourselves.

Those were very trying times for our family. My father was still in prison, and the never-ending strike cycle kept us kids out of school for nearly a year. My uncles, religious leaders, and seemingly everyone else believed it was their responsibility to chastise me. They held me to very high standards because I was Sheikh Hassan Yousef's firstborn son.

When I didn't live up to their expectations, they beat me. It didn't matter what I did, even going to the mosque five times a day, it was never enough.

I was sprinting around the mosque with a friend when the imam chased me down. When he seized me, he hoisted me over his head and slammed me onto my back on the floor. It took my breath away, and I thought I was going to die. Then he continued punching and kicking me. Why? I wasn't doing anything different than any of the other youngsters. But, as Hassan Yousef's son, I was expected to be better than that.

I had a friend whose father was a religious leader and Hamas power broker. This man was known for encouraging people to throw stones. While it was OK for other men's sons to be shot for pelting settlers with rocks, it was not acceptable for his only son. When he saw we were throwing stones, he summoned us to his home. We assumed he wanted to speak with us. However, he ripped the rope from a space heater and began whipping us with all his strength till we bled. He shattered our bond in trying to save his son, but my friend eventually left home, despising his father more than the devil.

No one supported our family while my father was in prison, except from attempting to keep me in line. We lost the extra money he earned teaching at the Christian school as a result of his arrest. The school promised to keep his work for him until his release, but we didn't have enough money to buy what we needed in the meantime.

I suppose no one assisted us because everyone assumed our family had a lot of money. After all, my father was a well-known religious and political figure. People undoubtedly believed that our extended relatives would assist us. Allah would undoubtedly provide. Our uncles, however, disregarded us. Allah took no action. So my mother had to care for her seven children on her own (our younger brother Mohammad had arrived in 1987).

Finally, when circumstances became desperate, my mother approached a friend of my father's for a loan—not to go shopping and purchase clothes and cosmetics for herself, but to feed her children at least one meal a day. But he turned her down. Instead of assisting us, he informed his Muslim friends that my mother had approached him begging for money.

I left as normal one winter day to sell my sweets. But when I arrived at the location, it was deserted. Because it was so cold, no one had come to work that day. My hands were cold, and it had begun to rain. I observed a car with numerous passengers parked on the side of the street while holding the plastic-covered tray over my head as an umbrella. When the driver noticed me, he opened his window and leaned out.

When I looked inside, I was surprised to find my uncle Ibrahim. His friends were surprised to see Ibrahim's nephew almost begging on a chilly, rainy day, and I was embarrassed to be an embarrassment to my uncle. I was at a loss for words. They, too, did not.

My uncle purchased all of the baklava, ordered me to go home, and promised to meet me later. He was furious with my mother when he arrived at our place. I couldn't hear what he said to her, but she was crying when he went. After school the next day, I changed and informed my mom I was ready to go back out to sell pastries.

Her eyes welled up with tears. I never went out again after that.

I was furious. I couldn't understand why our neighbours and family weren't willing to assist us. On top of that, they had the audacity to judge us for attempting to help ourselves. I questioned whether the actual reason they wouldn't help our family was because they were terrified of getting into problems if the Israelis felt they were assisting terrorists. However, we were not terrorists. My father was neither. Unfortunately, that would also alter.

Chapter 5: A Hero's Return

After being boycotted for a year and a half, our family was suddenly treated like royalty when my father was eventually released. The hero was back. I was no longer the black sheep, but the heir apparent. My brothers were princes, my sisters were princesses, and my mother reigned supreme. No one dared to pass judgement on us any longer.

In addition to his employment at the mosque, my father was rehired at the Christian school. My father attempted to help my mother around the house as much as he could now that he was home. This lightened the strain we kids were bearing. We weren't wealthy, but we had enough money to buy excellent food and even an occasional gift for the Stars winner. And we were well-endowed with honour and respect. The best part was that my father was with us. Nothing further was required.

Everything quickly resumed normalcy. Normal, of course, is a relative term. We were still under Israeli rule, with daily street killings. Our residence was only down the road from a gruesome corpse-filled graveyard. Our father had vivid memories of the Israeli prison where he had been held as a suspected terrorist for eighteen months. And the conquered regions had devolved into little more than a chaotic jungle.

One afternoon, I was playing indoors with my buddies when we heard screams outside. Fighting and yelling were nothing unusual in our society, but when we hurried outside, we noticed our neighbour, Abu Saleem, brandishing a large knife. He was attempting to murder his cousin, who was attempting to evade the gleaming sword as it cut through the air. The entire community attempted to stop Abu Saleem, but he was massive. He was a butcher by trade, and I once saw him slaughter a bull in his garden, leaving him covered in sticky, hot blood from head to foot. As I watched him race after his cousin, I couldn't help but think about what he'd done to that animal.

We informed my father what had happened when he got home that night. My father is barely five feet seven inches tall and not particularly athletic.

Abu Saleem, like everyone else, admired my father. Even in such circumstances, he had faith in his own expertise. He agreed to smooth things out with his cousin, and then he went to a meeting with the other men in the area with my father.

"Here is the situation," my father explained calmly. "We don't have a government here, and things are spiralling out of control." We can't keep fighting each other and shedding our own blood. We are fighting in the streets, in our homes, and in the mosques. Enough already. We'll need to sit down at least once a week and try to settle our problems like men. We don't have police, and there's no room for anyone to kill anyone. We have more pressing issues to address. I desire your cooperation. I want you to assist one another. We should act more like a family."

What my father was proposing made sense to the men. They agreed to meet every Thursday night to discuss local issues and resolve any disagreements they might have with one another.

My father's responsibility as imam of the mosque was to give people hope and to assist them in resolving their issues. He was also the closest thing to a government they had. He had turned into his father. But now he talked with Hamas' authority—with the authority of a sheikh. A sheikh wields greater power than an imam and is more akin to a general than a priest.

I had attempted to spend as much time as I could with my father since he had returned home three months prior. I was now the president of our school's Islamic student movement, and I wanted to learn everything I could about Islam and the study of the Qur'an. I asked if I may join him at the weekly neighbourhood gathering one Thursday evening. I said that I was almost a man and that I expected to be treated as such.

So he went away for a few hours. Someone knocked on the back door when my mother was preparing a lovely fish dinner. I opened the door just wide enough to see Captain Shai, the man who had arrested my father nearly two years before.

"Abuk mawjood?" "No, he's not here." "Then open the door."

I couldn't think of anything else to do, so I opened the door. Captain Shai was kind, as he had been the first time he came for my father, but he didn't believe me. When he asked if he might look around, I felt I had no choice but to let him. As the soldier began to search our home, moving from room to room, looking in closets and behind doors, I wished I could somehow prevent my father from returning home. I couldn't warn him because we didn't have a cell phone at the time. But the more I thought about it, the less I realised it would have mattered. He would have returned home anyhow.

We were regarded like refugees once more, even by the guys in the community he had sought to keep safe from themselves and others. Some individuals would express concern for my father, but it was evident to me that they didn't care.

Although we knew my father was imprisoned in Israel, no one would tell us which one. We spent three months searching for him in every prison until we learned he was being detained in a secret facility where only the most dangerous people are interrogated. I was curious as to why. Hamas had carried out no terrorist attacks. It was even unarmed.

When we discovered where my father was being detained, Israeli authorities allowed us to visit him once a month for thirty minutes. Because only two guests could enter at a time, we took turns accompanying our mother. When I first met him, I was astonished to see that he had let his beard grow long and that he appeared fatigued. Even so, it was wonderful to see him. He never grumbled. He merely wanted to know how things were going for us, and he wanted us to tell him everything.

During one of his visits, he offered me a bag of candy. He said that the prisoners were allotted one piece every other day, and instead of eating his, he had kept every piece for us. We kept the wrappers till the day he was released.

Finally, the long-awaited day arrived. We weren't expecting him, so when he strolled in, we all clung to him, frightened we were dreaming. People flocked to our residence for the following six hours once word of his arrival spread. We exhausted our storage tanks trying to offer everyone a sip of water because so many people came to greet him. I was proud as I observed the apparent regard and respect the people had for my father, but I was also upset. Where had everyone gone while he was gone?

"I am not working for these people, for their praise, or for them to take care of me and my family," my father said to me after everyone had departed. I am doing my best for Allah. And I know you're all paying just as much as I am. You, too, are Allah's servants, and you must be patient."

I got it, but I worried whether he realised how horrible things were when he wasn't there.

There was another knock at the back door while we were conversing. The Israelis detained him once more.

Chapter 6: Radical

Saddam Hussein attacked Kuwait in August 1990, while my father was in prison for the third time.

The Palestinians went insane. Everyone poured out into the streets, cheering and looking for the missiles that would undoubtedly fall on Israel. Our comrades had finally come to our aid! They planned to strike Israel square in the heart. The occupation would be finished soon.

Expecting another poison gas attack like the one that killed 5,000 Kurds in 1988, Israel issued gas masks to all citizens. However, each Palestinian home gets only one gas mask. My mother had one, but the seven of us didn't. So we experimented with making our own masks. In addition, we purchased nylon sheets and fastened them to the windows and doors. However, when we awoke the next morning, we discovered that the humidity had caused all of the tape to peel off.

We were glued to the Israeli TV channel, cheering with each warning of impending rockets. We climbed to the roof to watch the Iraqi Scuds light up Tel Aviv. But we didn't see anything.

I reasoned that Al-Bireh might not be the ideal position to obtain a nice view. I chose to visit my uncle Dawood's home at Al-Janiya, from where we could view all the way to the Mediterranean. Sohayb, my younger brother, accompanied me. The first rocket was visible from my uncle's roof. Actually, it was only the flame, but it was still a spectacular sight!

We were convinced that the administration was lying when we heard that around forty Scuds had reached Israel and just two Israelis had been killed. It turned out to be true. When the Iraqis modified the missiles to increase their range, they sacrificed power and accuracy.

We stayed at my uncle Dawood's house until Saddam Hussein was driven back to Baghdad by UN forces. I was enraged and deeply disappointed.

* * *

Following my father's release from the Persian Gulf War, my mother informed him that she wanted to sell her dowry gold in order to purchase a plot of land and obtain a loan to build our own home. Until this moment, we had been renting, and whenever my father was away, the owner defrauded us and became harsh and hostile to my mother.

My father was moved that she was willing to part with something so valuable, but he was also anxious that he would be unable to make the loan payments because he may be detained again at any time. Nonetheless, they decided to take a gamble, and in 1992, we built the house in Betunia, near Ramallah, where my family still resides today. I was fourteen years old.

My father was arrested again a few months after we moved. He was frequently not even charged with anything particular. Because we were under occupation, emergency rules empowered the Israeli government to arrest anyone solely on suspicion of involvement with terrorism. My father was an easy target because he was a religious—and, by extension, political—leader.

This appeared to be a pattern, and though we didn't realise it at the time, this pattern of arrest, release, and re-arrest would continue for many years to come, placing growing hardship on our family each time. Meanwhile, Hamas became increasingly militant and aggressive as younger Hamas men pushed the leadership to go even further.

The majority of attacks back then were personal, not organisational. Members with their own agendas had little authority over Hamas leaders. My father's goal was Islamic emancipation, and he believed that fighting Israel was the only way to accomplish it. Fighting, however, became its own objective for these young men—not a means to an end, but an end in itself.

The majority of the impatient young Hamas activists came from refugee camps. Imad Akel was one of them. Imad, the youngest of three kids, was training to be a pharmacist when he must have had enough of unfairness and frustration. He obtained a gun, murdered three Israeli troops, and stole their guns. Imad's influence rose as others followed in his footsteps. Imad formed his own military cell and relocated to the West Bank, where there were more targets and greater room to manoeuvre. I heard from the men in town that Hamas was quite proud of him, despite the fact that he was not at all answerable to the organisation. Nonetheless, the leaders did not want to confuse his actions with those of Hamas. So they established a military branch, the Ezzedeen Al-Qassam Brigades, and appointed Imad as its commander. He quickly became Israel's most wanted Palestinian.

Hamas had become armed. As weaponry swiftly replaced stones, graffiti, and Molotov cocktails, Israel was confronted with a challenge it had never seen before. Dealing with PLO attacks from Jordan, Lebanon, and Syria was one thing, but suddenly the attacks were coming from within its own borders.

Chapter 7: Fanning the Flames

Five Al-Qassam militants kidnapped Israeli border policeman Nissim Toledano near Tel Aviv on December 13, 1992. They called on Israel to release Sheikh Ahmed Yassin. Israel declined. Toledano's body was recovered two days later, and Israel initiated a tremendous crackdown on Hamas. More than 1600 Palestinians were arrested right away. Then Israel planned to deport 415 Hamas, Islamic Jihad, and Muslim Brotherhood officials in secret. My father, who was still in prison, and three uncles were among them.

I was just fourteen years old at the time, and none of us realised what was going on. As the news spread, we were able to piece together enough information to determine that my father was most likely among the huge group of teachers, religious leaders, engineers, and social workers who had been handcuffed, blindfolded, and loaded onto buses. Lawyers and human rights organisations began filing petitions within hours of the report surfacing. The buses were stopped until the Israeli High Court met at 5 a.m. to hear the legal challenges. My father and the other deportees were detained on the buses for the entire fourteen-hour argument. The blindfolds and handcuffs remained on. There is no food. There is no water. There will be no bathroom breaks. Finally, the court sided with the administration, and the buses resumed their journey north. The guys were then driven to a snow-covered no-man's land in southern Lebanon, we subsequently learned. Despite the fact that we were in the midst of a harsh winter, they were dumped there with no shelter or provisions. Neither Israel nor Lebanon would allow humanitarian organisations to transport food or medicine. Beirut refused to transport sick or injured people to its hospitals.

We waited nervously outside the Ramallah prison where the final deportees were to be freed on the specified day. The number ten was called. Twenty. He was not among them. The final man passed by, and the troops declared that was the end of it. My father was nowhere to be seen, and no one knew where he was. Other families joyfully escorted their loved ones home, leaving us standing outside alone in the middle of the night, unsure of where my father was. We returned home disheartened, annoyed, and concerned. Why hadn't he been released with the other inmates? What had happened to him?

My father's attorney contacted the next day to inform us that my father and several other deportees had been sent to prison. He claimed that the deportation had been harmful for Israel. During their exile, my father and other Palestinian leaders were all over the news, gaining sympathy from the international community since the punishment was seen as disproportionate and an abuse of their human rights. The guys were viewed as heroes of the cause throughout the Arab world, and as such, they became significantly more powerful and influential.

Another unanticipated but terrible consequence of the deportation was for Israel. The detainees exploited their exile to build an unparalleled partnership between Hamas and Hezbollah, Lebanon's dominant Islamic political and militant group. This link had significant historical and geopolitical implications. My father and other Hamas leaders frequently snuck out of the camp to meet with Hezbollah and Muslim Brotherhood leaders, something they could never do inside the Palestinian territory.

While my father and the others were in Lebanon, the most radical Hamas militants remained free and more enraged than ever. As these politicised young men assumed interim leadership positions within Hamas, the schism between Hamas and the PLO grew.

Around the same time, Israel and Yasser Arafat began covert talks, which resulted in the 1993 Oslo Accords. On September 9, Arafat sent a letter to Israeli Prime Minister Yitzhak Rabin in which he acknowledged "the right of the State of Israel to exist in peace and security" and condemned "the use of terrorism and other acts of violence."

During the Jewish holiday of Purim and the Muslim holy month of Ramadan, an American-born physician named Baruch Goldstein invaded Hebron's Al-Haram Al-Ibrahimi Mosque, where Adam and Eve, Abraham and Sarah, Isaac and Rebekah, and Jacob and Leah are said to be buried. Goldstein opened fire without warning, killing 29 Palestinians who had come to pray and injuring many more before being beaten to death by an irate, grief-stricken mob.

We sat and watched, via the lens of the television camera, as one bloodied corpse after another was dragged from that sacred site. I was taken aback. Everything appeared to go slowly. My heart hammered with a rage I'd never felt before, a rage that surprised and then comforted me. The next thing I knew, I was paralyzed with grief. Then I became enraged—then numb again. And I wasn't the only one. Everyone's emotions in the occupied territory seemed to rise and fall to that bizarre rhythm, leaving us tired.

A vehicle bomb exploded on a bus in Afula on April 6, killing eight people and wounding forty-four others. Hamas said it was in retaliation for Hebron. The same day, Hamas struck a bus stop outside Ashdod, killing two Israelis and injuring four more.

A week later, Israel had the first official suicide bombing, which marked a historic and terrible turning point. Amar Salah Diab Amarna, 21, arrived at the Hadera bus terminal in central Israel on Wednesday morning, April 13, 1994, the same day my father was finally released from prison after being deported to Lebanon. He was carrying a bag containing hardware as well as more than four pounds of homemade acetone peroxide explosive. He took the bus to Tel Aviv around 9:30 a.m. Ten minutes later, as the bus was leaving the station, he detonated the bag on the floor.

The shrapnel swept through the bus passengers, killing six and injuring thirty. Just as rescue workers arrived, a second pipe bomb exploded on the scene. According to a Hamas brochure, this was the "second in a series of five attacks" in retaliation for Hebron.

I was happy for Hamas, and I saw the strikes as a massive victory over Israel's occupation. I saw everything in black and white when I was fifteen years old. There were both nice and terrible people. And the bad guys deserved everything that happened to them. I witnessed what a two-kilogram bomb filled with nails and ball bearings could do to human flesh and hoped it would send a strong message to the Israeli population.

It did.

Pathologists frequently encouraged families not to view the remains, stating that it was preferable to remember their loved ones as they were when they were alive. Even if it was only a foot, most people wanted to touch the bodies one final time.

Larger body parts were frequently buried first since Jewish law mandated that the entire corpse be buried the same day a person died. Smaller bits were later added after DNA identification confirmed the identity, reopening the pain of mourning families.

While Hadera was the first recognized attack, it was actually the third attempt, part of a trial-and-error period in which Hamas bomb builder Yahya Ayyash honed his skills. Ayyash was a Birzeit University engineering student. He wasn't a fervent patriot or a radical Muslim. He was unhappy because he had once requested permission to pursue his studies in another country, and the Israeli government had denied his request. So he constructed bombs and became a Palestinian hero as well as one of Israel's most wanted individuals.

Ayyash would eventually be responsible for the deaths of at least 39 people in five further assaults, in addition to two unsuccessful attempts and the bombings on April 6 and 13. He also taught others, such as his friend Hassan Salameh, how to construct bombs.

* * *

Arafat was obligated by the Oslo Accords to form the Palestinian National Authority in the West Bank and Gaza Strip. So, on July 1, 1994, he approached Egypt's Rafah border, crossed into Gaza, and took up residence.

"National unity," he told the masses gathered to welcome him back from exile, "is... our shield, the shield of our people." "Unity, Unity, and Unity." However, the Palestinian lands were far from being unified.

Hamas and its followers were outraged that Arafat had met with Israel in secret and vowed that Palestinians would no longer fight for self-determination. Our men were still imprisoned in Israel. We didn't have a Palestinian state. The only authority we had was over Jericho, a small town with nothing, and Gaza, a large, overcrowded refugee camp on the coast.

Arafat was now sitting at the same table as the Israelis, shaking hands. "What about all the Palestinian blood?" our people wondered. "Did he hold it so cheap?"

Arafat made his first trip to Ramallah some months after arriving in Gaza. My father stood in a welcome line for him, along with dozens of religious, political, and business figures. When the PLO chief arrived at Sheikh Hassan Yousef's house, he kissed my father's hand, acknowledging him as both a religious and a political leader.

Over the next year, my father and other Hamas leaders met with Arafat frequently in Gaza City in an effort to reconcile and unite the PA and Hamas. However, the talks failed as Hamas refused to join in the peace process. Our philosophies and aspirations remained diametrically opposed.

* * *

Hamas had been transformed into a full-fledged terrorist organisation. Many of its members had ascended the Islamic ladder to the top. My father and other moderate political figures would not tell the extremists that what they were doing was wrong. They couldn't, so how could they say it was wrong? The militants had the full weight of the Qur'an behind them.

So, despite the fact that he had never directly killed anyone, my father supported the attacks. And, failing to locate and apprehend the aggressive young terrorists, Israel continued to pursue soft targets such as my father. They probably thought that because my father was a leader of Hamas, which was carrying out the assaults, his arrest would put an end to them. But they never bothered to find out who or what Hamas was. And it would take many painful years for them to realise that Hamas was not an organisation in the way most people understood organisations, with rules and a hierarchy. It was a spirit. A thought. An idea cannot be destroyed; it can only be stimulated. Hamas is like a flatworm. When you cut off its head, it immediately grows another.

The problem was that Hamas's primary organising concept and objective were deceptive. Syria, Lebanon, Iraq, Jordan, and Egypt had tried and failed numerous times to force Israelis into the sea and turn their lands into a Palestinian state. Saddam Hussein and his Scud rockets also failed. Millions of Palestinian refugees would have to virtually swap places with Israel in order to reclaim their homes, farms, and property lost more than a half-century ago. And because that was plainly not going to happen, Hamas was cursed to perpetually roll a rock up a steep hill, only to see it roll back down, never attaining the goal.

Even those who regarded Hamas's aim as impossible clung to the hope that Allah would one day vanquish Israel, even if he had to do so supernaturally.

The PLO nationalists were just a political problem in need of a political solution for Israel. Hamas, on the other hand, Islamized the Palestinian issue, turning it into a religious one. And this problem could only be handled religiously, which meant it could never be solved since we felt the land belonged to Allah. Period.

The discussion has come to an end. Thus, the ultimate difficulty for Hamas was not Israel's policies. It was the very reason for Israel's existence as a nation-state.

What about my father? Had he also become a terrorist? I read a newspaper headline one afternoon about a recent suicide bombing (or "martyrdom operation," as some in Hamas referred to it) that murdered numerous civilians, including women and children. It was impossible for me to reconcile my father's generosity and character, as well as his leadership, with an organisation that did such things. I showed him the paper and asked how he felt about such behaviour.

"Once," he explained, "I was leaving the house and there was an insect outside." I debated whether I should kill it or not. And I couldn't get rid of it." That evasive response was his way of stating that he could never personally participate in such heinous murder. The Israeli civilians, on the other hand, were not insects.

No, my father did not construct the bombs, strap them to the bombers, or choose the targets. Years later, when I came upon a tale in a Christian Bible about the stoning of a young innocent named Stephen, I remembered my father's response. It was written, "Saul was there, giving approval to his death" (Acts 8:1).

I adored my father and liked everything about him and what he stood for. But, for a man who couldn't bear the thought of harming an insect, he had evidently found a way to rationalise the idea that it was fine for someone else to blow up people into scraps of meat as long as he didn't get his hands bloodied.

My feelings for my father became considerably more conflicted at that point.

Chapter 8: Guns

The international community expected the Palestinian Authority to hold Hamas in control following the Oslo Accords. On Saturday, November 4, 1995, I was watching television when a news bulletin interrupted the show. Yitzhak Rabin was shot during a peace protest in Tel Aviv's Kings Square. It sounded solemn. He was declared deceased a few hours later by officials.

The phone then rang. I immediately recognized the caller's voice. Yasser Arafat called and asked to talk with my father.

As my father spoke into the phone, I listened. He didn't say much; he was polite and respectful, and he mainly agreed with whatever Arafat was saying on the other end of the phone.

We eventually discovered that Rabin had not been assassinated by a Palestinian after all. Instead, an Israeli law student shot him in the back. Many Hamas members were dismayed by this knowledge, but I found it hilarious that Jewish extremists shared a goal with Hamas.

I was seventeen years old and only a few months away from graduating from high school. When I visited my father in prison or brought him food from home and other comfort items, he encouraged me, saying, "All you have to do is pass your tests." Concentrate on your school. Don't be concerned about me. I don't want this to get in the way of anything." But life had lost its meaning for me. I couldn't think of anything else than joining Hamas' military wing and exacting revenge on Israel and the Palestinian Authority. I reflected on everything I had witnessed in my life. Was all of this labour and sacrifice going to end in a shambles with Israel? If I died fighting, at the very least I'd be a martyr and go to heaven.

I couldn't understand how he could be so kind and forgiving, even to the troops who came over and over to arrest him. He handled them as if they were children. When I delivered him lunch at the PA compound, he would frequently invite the guards to join us and enjoy my mother's specially made beef and rice. After a few months, even the PA guards were smitten with him. While it was easy to adore him, he was also a tough man to comprehend.

I began looking for guns because I was filled with rage and a desire for vengeance. Weapons were accessible in the territories by this time, but they were prohibitively expensive, and I was a student with no money.

Aside from desiring vengeance, I thought it would be nice to be a teenager with a gun. I had lost interest in school. Why would anyone go to school in this crazy country?

We knew better than to use words like firearms or weapons because the Israelis were likely listening to everything we said. We soon agreed on a time for Ibrahim to pick up his "things" and said good night.

The year was 1996, and it was spring. I had recently turned eighteen and was armed.

***

Ibrahim contacted me one night, and I could tell by the tone of his voice that he was furious.

He yelled into the phone, "The guns don't work!"

"What are you talking about?" I replied, praying no one was listening in on our talk.

"The guns don't work," he said again. "We were cheated!" "I can't talk right now," I explained.

"Okay, but I want to see you tonight."

I instantly lit into him when he came to my house. "Are you crazy, talking like that on the phone?" I asked.

"I understand, but the guns aren't working." The handgun is fine, but the submachine guns would not fire."

"All right, they're not working. "Are you certain you understand how to use them?" He assured me that he knew exactly what he was doing, so I told him I'd handle it. I didn't have time for any of this because my final exams were only two weeks away, but I went ahead and made the arrangements to return the defective pistols to Yousef.

"This is a disaster," I said as soon as I saw him. "The handgun is functional, but the machine guns are not." Please contact your Nablus contacts so that we can at least get our money back." He pledged to give it his best shot.

My brother Sohayb broke the bad news to me the next day. "Israeli security forces came to the house last night, looking for you," he said, his voice anxious.

My initial impression was, "We haven't even killed anyone yet!" I was terrified, but I also felt important, as if I was becoming a threat to Israel. When I went to see my father the next time, he had already heard that the Israelis were looking for me.

"What's going on?" he said solemnly. When I told him the truth, he became enraged. However, it was evident from his rage that he was mostly disappointed and anxious.

"This is very serious," he said. "How did you get yourself into this mess?" You should be looking after your mother and siblings and sisters, not fleeing the Israelis. "Don't you realise they're going to shoot you?"

I went home, threw on some clothing and schoolbooks, and begged several Muslim Brotherhood students to hide me until my exams and graduation.

Ibrahim plainly didn't get the gravity of my situation. He kept calling, often on my father's cell phone.

"What exactly is going on?" What is going on with you? I gave you the entire sum. "I require its return."

When I told him about the security guys who had come to my house, he began to yell and say irresponsible things on the phone. I hurriedly hung up before he could further involve himself or me. However, the IDF arrived at his house the next day, searched it, and discovered the weapon. They arrested him right away.

I was disoriented. I had placed my trust in someone I should not have. My father was in prison and was dissatisfied with me. My mother was concerned about me. I had examinations to prepare for. And the Israelis wanted me.

What could possibly go wrong now?

Chapter 9: The Slaughterhouse

Despite my best efforts, the Israeli security agents caught up with me. They had eavesdropped on my chats with Ibrahim, and now I was shackled and blindfolded, jammed in the back of a military jeep, dodging rifle butts as best I could.

The jeep came to a halt. We'd been on the road for what seemed like hours. As the soldiers seized me by my arms and hauled me up a flight of steps, the handcuffs cut severely into my wrists. I couldn't feel my hands anymore. I could hear people moving and shouting in Hebrew all around me.

My blindfold and handcuffs were removed as I was led into a small room. I squinted in the dim light to establish my bearings. The room was empty save for a little desk in the corner. I was curious as to what the military had in store for me next. Interrogation? More thrashings? Torture? I didn't have to think about it for long. A young soldier opened the door after only a few minutes. He had a nose ring, and I recognized his Russian accent. He was one of the soldiers who had beaten me in the jeep's back seat. He took my arm and led me down a long, winding path and into another little room. An antique desk had a blood pressure cuff and monitor, a computer, and a small TV. As I walked in, an overwhelming stink overwhelmed my nostrils. I gagged, certain that I was ready to vomit again.

Behind us, a man in a doctor's coat entered, looking worn and unhappy. He was taken aback when he saw my damaged face and swollen eye, which had grown to twice its original size. But if he was worried about my well-being, he didn't show it. I'd seen veterinarians who were more gentle with their patients than this guy was as he checked me.

A police officer in a uniform entered. He spun me around, reapplied the handcuffs, and pulled a dark green hood over my head. I'd discovered the source of the stink. The hood smelled as if it had never been cleaned. It smelled like a hundred inmates' unbrushed teeth and bad breath. I wretched and struggled to keep my breath. I sucked the filthy fabric into my lips every time I gasped. I panicked and thought I was going to suffocate if I couldn't break out from the bag.

The guard searched me and took everything from me, including my belt and bootlaces. He grabbed my hood and dragged me down the corridors. A left turn. A left. Another person walked away. Right. Once again, you are correct. I had no idea where I was or where he was leading me.

We eventually came to a halt, and I heard him fumble for a key. He pushed open a big and heavy door. "Steps," he explained. I also felt my way down a few treads. I could see a flashing light through the hood, similar to what you'd see on the top of a police car.

When the guard removed his hood, I noticed I was standing in front of a set of curtains. I noticed a basket of hoods to my right. We waited a few moments until a voice from the other side of the curtain let us enter. The soldier shackled my ankles and placed my head into another bag. He then grabbed the front and dragged me through the drapes.

Music erupted from somewhere in the distance as cold air poured out of the vents. I must have been travelling down an extremely narrow corridor because I kept collapsing against the walls on either side. I was dizzy and tired. Finally, we came to a halt. The soldier pushed me inside after opening a door. He then removed the hood and walked away, closing the heavy door behind him.

I took another glance around, examining my surroundings. The cage was approximately six feet square, with just enough space for a modest mattress and two blankets. One of them had been rolled into a pillow by whoever had occupied the cell before me. I sat down on the mattress, which was sticky and smelled like the hood. My garments reeked of vomit, so I covered my nose with the collar of my shirt. I could see one dim light bulb hanging from the ceiling but couldn't find the switch to turn it on or off. The sole window in the room was a small aperture in the door. The air was clammy, the floor was moist, and the concrete was mouldy. There were bugs everywhere. Everything was nasty, rotten, and unsightly.

I sat there for a long time, unsure what to do. I needed to use the restroom and stood in the corner to use the rusted toilet. I pushed the flush handle and quickly regretted it. Instead of flushing the excrement, it poured out onto the floor and soaked into the mattress.

I sat in the room's only dry corner and tried to think. What a wonderful place to spend the night! My eyes were throbbing and burning. It was difficult for me to breathe without choking on the odour of the place. My sweat-soaked garments clung to my frame as the heat in my cage became unbearable.

I hadn't eaten or drunk anything since my mother's goat's milk. And it was now all over my shirt and pants. I turned the lever on a pipe protruding from the wall, hoping to draw some water from it. The liquid turned out to be thick and brown.

What was the time? Were they planning on leaving me here all night?

My head was pounding. I knew I wouldn't be able to sleep that night. I had no choice but to pray to Allah.

I requested that you protect me. Keep me safe and return me to my family as soon as possible.

I could hear loud music playing in the distance through the heavy steel door—the same tape, over and over and over. The mind-numbing repetitions helped me keep track of time.

Many doors opened and closed in the distance. The sounds got closer and closer. Then someone opened my cell door, pushed a blue dish inside, and slammed it shut. I looked down at the tray, which was sitting in the sewage that had flowed out of the toilet after I used it. One boiled egg, a solitary piece of toast, a teaspoon of sour-smelling yoghurt, and three olives were among its contents. A plastic water jug sat off to the side, but when I brought it to my lips, it didn't smell right. I drank a small amount and used the remainder to wash my hands. Despite eating everything on the tray, I was still hungry. Was this your breakfast? What was the time? I assumed midday.

The door to my cell opened while I was still attempting to figure out how long I had been there. Someone or something stood there. Was it a person? He was short, appeared to be around 75 years old, and resembled a hunchbacked ape. He cursed me, cursed God, and spat in my face, all with a Russian accent. I couldn't think of anything more repulsive.

This monster must have been a guard, since he thrust another nasty hood at me and told me to put it over my head. Then he seized the front and yanked me into the corridors. He pushed me into an office, slammed me down onto a low plastic chair that felt like a small child's chair from an elementary school classroom. The chair was securely fastened to the floor.

He had me shackled, one arm between the chair legs, the other outside. Then he bound my legs. I had to lean forward because the small seat was sloped. This room, unlike my confinement, was bitterly chilly. I reasoned that the air conditioning must be set around zero.

I remained there for hours, trembling uncontrollably in the cold, bent at a painful angle, unable to change positions. I attempted to breathe through the foul bag without taking a complete breath. I was starving, tired, and my eye was still swollen with blood.

When the door opened, someone removed my hood. I was astonished to see that it wasn't a soldier or a guard. He perched on the desk's edge. My head was roughly the same height as his knees.

Did he truly believe I was that dangerous? That seemed unbelievable to me. But the more I thought about it, the more I realised he probably did. His mistrust was heightened by the fact that I was the son of Sheikh Hassan Yousef and was purchasing automatic firearms.

These men had imprisoned and tortured my father before torturing me. Did they honestly assume that by doing so, I would accept their right to exist? My viewpoint was quite different. My people were fighting for our liberty and our nation.

When I did not respond to his questions, he pounded his fist against the desk. He lifted my chin once more.

"I'm going to spend the night with my family at home." You're having a good time here." I sat on the little chair for hours, awkwardly leaning forward. Finally, a guard entered the room, unlocked my handcuffs and chains, slapped another hood over my head, and dragged me back through the halls. Leonard Cohen's voice became increasingly audible.

We came to a halt, and the guard motioned for me to sit down. The music was becoming deafening. I was once again shackled hand and foot to a low chair that shook to the relentless beat of "First we take Manhattan, then we take Berlin!"

My muscles were cramping as a result of the cold, uncomfortable position. I could smell the odour of the hood. However, I was certainly not alone this time. I could hear other people crying out in agony over Leonard Cohen.

Every minute felt like an hour, but I couldn't remember what an hour was in the first place. My world had come to a halt. Outside, I could see individuals getting up, going to work, and returning home to their families. My classmates were revising for final examinations. My mother was cooking, cleaning, and hugging and loving my younger siblings.

But everyone sat in that room. Nobody moved.

We start in Manhattan and then go on to Berlin! We start in Manhattan and then go on to Berlin! We start in Manhattan and then go on to Berlin!

Some of the men surrounding me sobbed, but I refused to cry. My father had never cried, I was certain. He was powerful. He refused to give in.

I was completely weary and sick to my stomach. My neck hurts. I had no idea how heavy my head was. I tried to lean against the wall next to me, but just as I was about to fall asleep, a guard came up behind me and smacked me in the head to wake me up. His whole purpose seemed to be to keep us awake and silent. After answering incorrectly, I felt as if I had been buried alive and was being tortured by the angels Munkar and Nakir.

It had to be dawn because I heard a guard moving around. He opened handcuffs and shackles one by one and led individuals away. He brought them back after a few minutes, tied them to the tiny seats again, and moved on to the next one. He eventually came to me.

He seized my hood and dragged me into the corridors after unlocking my chains. He directed me to enter a cell and opened the door. When he lowered the hood, I saw the same hunchbacked, apelike guard who had guarded my food. With his foot, he pushed the blue plate containing an egg, toast, yoghurt, and olives toward me. Nearly an inch of filthy water splattered on the floor and into the tray. I'd rather have gone hungry than eaten it.

"You have two minutes to eat and use the toilet," he said.

I just wanted to stretch, lie down, and sleep for two minutes. But I just remained there, watching the seconds pass.

"Come on, come on!" "Come on in!"

Before I could eat, the guard drew the bag over my head, led me back through the halls, and shackled me to the small chair.

We start in Manhattan and then go on to Berlin!

Chapter 10: The Offer

Doors opened and closed all day as captives were dragged from one interrogator to the next by their dirty hoods. Uncuffed, cuffed, interrogated, and thrashed. An interrogator would occasionally shake a prisoner violently. He generally passed out after barely ten shakes. Uncuffed, cuffed, and interrogated. Doors were opened and closed.

Every morning, we were escorted for our two-minute blue breakfast tray, followed by our two-minute orange supper tray a few hours later. After hour after hour. Day in and day out. Breakfast tray in blue. Dinner tray in orange. I rapidly started to look forward to mealtimes, not because I wanted to eat, but because it gave me the opportunity to stand up straight.

The opening and closing of doors ceased at night after we had all been fed. The interrogators left. The business day had come to an end. And so the never-ending night began. People sobbed, moaned, and yelled. They no longer sounded like people. Some had no idea what they were saying. Muslims recite Quranic passages, pleading with Allah for strength. I prayed as well, but I received no strength. I reflected on dumb Ibrahim, stupid firearms, and stupid phone calls to my father's cell phone.

I remembered my father. My heart ached as I realised what he must have gone through while imprisoned. But I was familiar with my father's personality. Even while being tormented and humiliated, he would have silently and willingly accepted his fate. He most likely became friends with the guards who were in charge of the beatings. He would have shown genuine interest in them as individuals, inquiring about their families, backgrounds, and hobbies.

My routine was unexpectedly disrupted one day. A guard entered the cell and untied me from my chair. I knew it was far too early for dinner, but I didn't inquire. I was willing to travel anywhere, even to hell, if it meant getting out of that chair. I was led to a small office and shackled again, this time to an ordinary chair. When a Shin Bet officer entered the room, he looked me over. Though the pain wasn't as intense as it had been, I knew the marks from the soldiers' rifle butts were still visible on my face.

I could tell Loai thought I was incredibly scary. I understood from speaking with others who had spent time in Israeli jails that Palestinians were not often treated as cruelly as I had been. They were not all interrogated for so long.

What I didn't realise at the time was that Hassan Salameh had been detained about the same time as me.

Salameh has carried out a number of strikes in retaliation for the killing of master bomb maker Yahya Ayyash. When the Shin Bet overheard me discussing weaponry with Ibrahim on my father's cell phone, they suspected I wasn't working alone. They were certain I had been recruited by Al-Qassam.

I began to cry. I had wished for a human being to chat to while in prison. A member of my own family was now yelling at me from the opposite side of the wall. Then it hit me: the Israelis were listening; they had placed Yousef right next to me so they could listen in on our chat and see if I was telling the truth. That was perfectly great with me. I told Yousef that I needed the guns to protect my family, so I wasn't concerned.

When the Shin Bet realised my story was true, they moved me to a different jail. Alone once again, I reflected on how I had ruined my cousin's life, hurt my family, and squandered twelve years of education—all because I had trusted a jerk like Ibrahim!

I was locked up for weeks with no human interaction. The guards put food under the door but said nothing to me. I even started missing Leonard Cohen. I had nothing to read, and the daily rotation of coloured food trays was my only way of passing the time. There is nothing to do but think and pray.

Finally, one day, I was led to an office, where Loai was waiting to speak with me.

"If you decide to cooperate with us, Mosab, I will do my best to see that you don't have to spend more time in prison."

A ray of hope. Maybe I can trick him into thinking I'm going to cooperate, and then he'll let me out of here.

I was still disgusted by everything around me. The profession. The PA. I had become a radical solely for the purpose of destroying something. But it was that urge that had put me into this problem in the first place. I was in an Israeli jail, and now this man was urging me to work for them. I knew that if I answered yes, I would have to pay a horrible price—both in this life and the next.

"Okay, I need to think about it," I heard myself say.

I returned to my cell and considered Loai's proposition. I'd heard of folks who accepted to work for the Israelis but turned out to be double agents. They assassinated their handlers, hid weapons, and took advantage of any opportunity to inflict further harm on the Israelis. If I said yes, I figured Loai would probably let me go. He'd probably even offer me the opportunity to have actual weapons this time, and I'd kill him with them.

The flames of hatred raged within me. I sought vengeance on the soldier who had brutally beaten me. I desired vengeance on Israel. I didn't care about the price, even if it meant losing my life.

However, working for the Shin Bet would be far riskier than purchasing guns. I should probably simply forget about it, finish my sentence in prison, go home and study, be near my mother, and look after my siblings and sisters.

The guard took me back to the office one more time the next day, and Loai came in a few minutes later.

They returned me to my cell, where I remained for the next few weeks. I couldn't wait to leave Maskobiyeh. The guard finally told me it was time to leave one morning. He tied me again, but this time I had my hands in front of me. There is no hood. I saw the light and felt the outside air for the first time in 45 days. I inhaled deeply, filling my lungs and enjoying the breeze on my face. I hopped into the rear of a Ford van and sat in the passenger seat. I didn't care that it was a hot summer day and the metal seat I was shackled to was burning. I felt liberated!

We got to Megiddo Prison two hours later, but we had to wait in the van for another hour for permission to enter. Once inside, a prison doctor examined me and declared that I was alright. I was given clean clothes and toiletries after taking a shower with real soap. For the first time in weeks, I ate hot food at lunch.

I was asked which group I belonged to. "Hamas," I replied.

Every organisation was authorised to police its own individuals in Israeli prisons. The objective was that this would either alleviate some of the social issues or increase conflict among the factions. If the prisoners directed their rage toward one another, they would have less energy to fight the Israelis.

All prisoners were asked to disclose their affiliation upon entering a new prison. We had to pick a side: Hamas, Fatah, Islamic Jihad, the Popular Front for the Liberation of Palestine (PFLP), the Democratic Front for the Liberation of Palestine (DFLP), or anything. We couldn't simply claim to be nothing. Prisoners who were nothing in particular would be allowed a few days to choose an organisation. Inside the prison at Megiddo, Hamas had complete power. Hamas was the largest and most powerful group in the region. Hamas set the rules, and everyone else followed them.

When I walked in, the other inmates greeted me warmly, slapping my back and congratulating me on entering the ranks. We sat about in the evening and told each other stories. But after a while, I started to feel a little uneasy. One of the guys seemed to be a leader for the detainees, and he was asking too many questions. I didn't trust him, even though he was the emir—the Hamas authority within the prison. I'd heard a lot of stories about "birds," which are prison spies.

Why doesn't he trust me if he's a Shin Bet spy, I wondered? Now I'm meant to be one of them. I decided to play it safe and say nothing more than what I had told the detention facility interrogators.

I spent two weeks at Megiddo Prison praying, fasting, and reading the Qur'an. When fresh inmates arrived, I warned them about the emir.

Yeah, and I'll shoot you in the head one day, I thought as I watched him walk away. I felt pleased with myself for having such daring ideas.

I stayed at the detention centre for another twenty-five days, but this time I was in a cell with three other convicts, including my cousin Yousef. We passed the time by conversing and sharing anecdotes. One of the guys informed us about how he had killed someone. Another boasted about dispatching suicide bombers. Everyone had a fascinating story to tell. We sat around praying, singing, and having a good time. Anything to divert our attention away from our existing surroundings. It was not a safe haven for humanity.

Except for my cousin, we were all transferred to Megiddo. But this time we weren't siding with the birds; we were on our way to a real prison. Nothing would ever be the same after that.

Chapter 11: Number 823

They could sense our approach.

After three months of not using scissors or razors, our hair and beards were lengthy. Our clothing was filthy. It took roughly two weeks to get rid of the detention centre's stench. Scrubbing was ineffective. It simply had to wear off.

The mi'var, a facility where everyone was processed before being sent to the greater camp population, was where the majority of the inmates began their term. Some convicts, however, were deemed too dangerous to be released into the general community and spent years in the mi'var. Unsurprisingly, all of these males were Hamas supporters. Some of the guys recognized me and approached us to say hello.

I was used to being recognized everywhere I went as Sheikh Hassan's son. If he was the king, I was the prince—the obvious heir. And I was treated accordingly.

"We heard you were in town around a month ago. Your uncle has arrived. He'll pay you a visit soon."

Lunch was hot and satisfying, although not quite as good as what I had eaten with the birds. Still, I was content. Even though I was in prison, I felt liberated. When I got some alone time, I thought about the Shin Bet. I had committed to collaborate with them, but they had not communicated with me. They never specified how we would communicate or what it meant to collaborate. They simply abandoned me with no instructions on how to act. I was really lost. I had forgotten who I was. I began to wonder if I had been duped.

Every morning at four o'clock, we were roused to prepare for pre-dawn prayer. We stood in line with our towels, looking like men first thing in the morning and smelling like men when there aren't any fans or ventilation. Then it was wudu time. We washed our hands up to the wrist, rinsed our lips, and smelt water into our nostrils to begin the Islamic ritual of purification. We cleaned our faces with both hands from forehead to chin and ear to ear, washed our arms up to our elbows, and wiped our heads once with a wet hand from the forehead to the back of the neck. Finally, we wiped our ears inside and out, wiped around our necks, and cleansed both feet up to the ankles with wet fingers. The technique was then done two more times.

When everyone had finished, the imam—a burly, tough guy with a thick beard—chanted the adhan at 4:30. Then he recited Al-Fatihah (the first sura, or portion, from the Qur'an), and we proceeded through four rakats (repetitions of prayers as well as standing, kneeling, and bending postures).

Because the majority of us were Muslims linked with Hamas or Islamic Jihad, this was our normal routine. Even members of secular and communist organisations were required to rise at the same time, even if they did not pray. And they were furious about it.

Because he was unarmed, we sat on our bunks with our backs to the Israeli soldier who counted us. He only took five minutes, and we were permitted to go back to sleep.

We reviewed the rules for reading the Qur'an at the first Hamas jalsa of the day. All of what I had learned from my father, but most convicts had no idea. The second daily jalsa was more about Hamas, our own discipline inside the prison, new arrival notifications, and news from outside. There are no secrets or plans, only broad information.

We often passed the time after each jalsa by watching television on the set at the far end of the room, opposite the toilets. I was watching a cartoon one morning when an ad came on.

BANG!

In front of the television, a large wooden board swung down. I took a step back and looked around.

Of course, not everyone saw it in the same light. What we were able to see was heavily influenced by who held the rope. If the guy was from Hebron, he'd drop the board to cover even a female cartoon character who wasn't wearing a scarf; if he was from liberal Ramallah, we'd see a lot more. We were supposed to take turns holding the rope, but I wouldn't touch it.

After lunch, there was another quiet time, followed by noontime prayer. During this period, the majority of the inmates napped. Normally, I read a book. And in the evenings, we were allowed to go for a walk or just hang out and talk in the workout area.

For Hamas members, prison life was tedious. We weren't permitted to play cards. We were required to read just the Qur'an and Islamic texts. The other groups were given far more leeway than we were.

The year was 1996, and it was the summer. Despite the fact that I was just eighteen, I felt as if I had lived several lifetimes in a matter of months. A few weeks after my uncle's visit, a prisoner representative, or shaweesh, entered Room Nine and exclaimed, "Eight twenty-three!" I raised my head, astonished to hear my phone number. He then shouted out three or four more numbers and instructed us to gather our items.

The heat hit me like dragon's breath as we stepped out of the mi'var onto the desert, making me dizzy for a time. Nothing except the tops of large brown tents stretched ahead of us for as far as I could see. We marched through the first, second, and third sections. Hundreds of inmates rushed to the high chain-link fence to see the newcomers. When we got to Section Five, the gates swung open. Over fifty individuals surrounded us, hugged us, and shook our hands.

I was allocated to the Hamas tent in Quadrant One's upper right corner, third bunk on the right. We were all gathered around discussing after the first head count when a distant voice cried, "Bareed ya mujahideen! [Mail from the liberation warriors! Mail!] says Bareed.

It was the sawa'ed in the following part that gave everyone a heads up. The sawa'ed were Hamas security wing agents within the prison who relayed communications from one part to the next. The name was derived from the Arabic term for "throwing arms."

When they heard the cry, two guys ran out of their tents, held out their palms, and looked up at the sky. A ball appeared out of nowhere and fell into their waiting hands, as if on cue. This was how Hamas officials in our sector received encrypted commands or information from other sections' leaders. This means of communication was employed by every Palestinian organisation in the prison. Each had its own code name, so when the warning was yelled, the right "catchers" knew to dash into the drop zone.

Bread softened with water was used to make the balls. After inserting the message, the dough was rolled into a softball-sized ball, dried, and hardened. Only the greatest pitchers and catchers were chosen as "postmen."

The thrill was gone as fast as it had begun. It was then time for lunch.

Chapter 12: Trust No One

It felt great to see the sky after being trapped down for so long. It seemed like I hadn't seen the stars in years. Despite the large camp lights that diminished their brightness, they were stunning. But the arrival of the stars signalled that it was time to return to our tents and prepare for head count and bed. That's when things became quite perplexing for me.

My prisoner number was 823, and we were billeted in sequential order. That meant I'd be sent to the Hamas tent in Quadrant Three. But that tent was filled, so I was given to the Quadrant One corner tent.

However, when it came time for the head count, I still had to stand in the proper location in Quadrant Three. That way, when the guard went down his list, he wouldn't have to recall all of the housekeeping changes he'd made to keep things tidy.

Every headcount movement was choreographed.

Twenty-five men entered Quadrant One, M16s at the ready, and then moved from tent to tent. We were all facing the canvas with our backs to the army. For fear of being shot, no one dared to move.

When they were done there, the soldiers proceeded to Quadrant Two. They then closed both gates in the fence, preventing anyone from One or Two from sneaking into Three or Four to cover for a missing prisoner.

On my first night in Section Five, I witnessed a strange kind of shell game going on. When I first entered Three, a sickly-looking prisoner stood next to me. He appeared horrifying, almost as if he were ready to die. He had his head shaved and was plainly fatigued. He never looked me in the eyes. What happened to this guy, and who is he? I was perplexed.

When the soldiers concluded the first head count and proceeded on to the second, someone seized the guy and hauled him out of the tent, and another prisoner took his place next to me. Later, I discovered that a small hole had been created in the fence between One and Three so that the prisoner might be swapped with someone else.

Nobody, obviously, wanted the soldiers to see the bald person. But why is this so?

That night, as I lay in my bed, I heard someone moaning in the distance, evidently in a lot of pain. It didn't last long, though, and I quickly fell asleep.

Morning usually arrived too quickly, and we were woken up for pre-dawn prayer before I knew it. 140 of the 240 inmates in Section Five stood in line to use the six toilets—actually six holes with privacy barriers over a shared pit. There are eight wudu basins. It takes thirty minutes.

Then we formed rows for prayer. The daily regimen was nearly identical to that of the mi'var. However, there were now twelve times as many convicts. Even with that many people, I was surprised at how effortlessly everything went. Nobody seemed to make a mistake. It was almost unsettling.

Everyone appeared to be afraid. Nobody ventured to break a rule. Nobody dared to linger too long at the toilet. No one dared to make eye contact with a detained suspect or an Israeli soldier. Nobody was ever too close to the fence.

It didn't take long for me to realise what was going on. Hamas was running its own performance behind the nose of the jail authorities, and they were keeping score. When you break a rule, you get a red point. Collect enough red points, and you'd be reporting to the maj'd, Hamas' security wing—tough individuals who didn't smile or make jokes.

We didn't see the maj'd very often because they were too busy gathering intelligence. The message balls that were hurled from one section to the next were from and for them.

I was sitting on my bed one day when the maid walked in and said, "Everybody evacuate this tent!" Nobody said anything. The tent was gone in an instant. They escorted a man into the now-empty tent, shut the flap, and stationed two guards. Someone turned on the television. Loud. Other men began to sing and make noises.

I had no idea what was going on inside the tent, but I'd never heard a human cry like that before. What could he possibly have done to deserve it? I was perplexed. The torment lasted around thirty minutes. Then two majors led him out and into another tent, where the interrogation resumed.

When we were evacuated, I was talking to a buddy named Akel Sorour, who was from a hamlet near Ramallah. Because Israel had been so successful in locating and imprisoning Hamas cells, the maj'd felt that the organisation must be filled with spies, and they were desperate to expose them. They were watching everything we did. They observed our demeanour and listened intently to everything we said. They then counted the points. We knew who they were but not who their spies were. Someone I believed was a friend could be working with the maj'd, and I could be probed tomorrow.

I determined that keeping to myself as much as possible and being cautious about who I trusted was my best hope. My life changed significantly once I realised the camp's environment of suspicion and deceit. I felt as if I were in a different prison, one where I couldn't walk freely, communicate freely, trust, relate, or befriend. I was frightened of making a mistake, being late, sleeping through wake-up calls, or falling asleep during jalsa.

I spent my days duplicating prisoner dossiers. We took great care to keep this information out of the hands of prison officials. We never used names, only codes. The files, written on the thinnest paper possible, read like the worst type of erotica. Guys admitted to having sex with their mothers. One claimed he had sex with a cow. Another had sexual relations with his daughter. Another had intercourse with his neighbour, filmed it with a spy camera, and then handed the photos over to the Israelis. According to the claim, the Israelis gave the neighbour the photos and threatened to transmit them to her family if she refused to collaborate with their spy. So they continued to have sex together, collect information, and have sex with others while filming it, until the entire hamlet appeared to be working for the Israelis. And this was only the first file I was requested to duplicate.

It felt insane to me. As I continued to duplicate the data, I understood that tortured suspects were being asked questions they couldn't possibly know about and delivering replies their torturers wanted to hear. They appeared to be willing to say anything to end the pain. I also thought that some of these odd interrogations served no purpose other than to feed the imprisoned majid's sexual fantasies.

Our family was allowed to see us once a month. Because Israeli prison cuisine was lacking, they regularly sent us homemade food and personal items. Our families arrived on the same day because Akel and I were from the same area.

The Red Cross gathered family members from a certain area and placed them onto buses after a lengthy application process. Megiddo was only a two-hour drive away. However, because the buses had to stop at each checkpoint and all passengers had to be checked, our family had to leave the house at four a.m. in order to arrive at the prison by noon.

Ibrahim Abu Salem sat with the maj'd, laughing and eating the meal

Akel's sister had brought for her imprisoned brother. Nearby, fellow Hamas members—Arabs, Palestinians, and Muslims—pushed needles beneath Akel's fingernails.

Over the next few weeks, I only saw Akel a few times. His head and beard had been shaved, and his gaze was fixed on the ground. He was frail and appeared like an old man on the verge of death.

I was later handed his file to copy. He admitted to having sex with all of the women in his hamlet, as well as donkeys and other animals. I knew every line was a fraud, yet I duplicated the file and mailed it to the maj's village. His sister had abandoned him. His peers avoided him.

The maj'd were far worse than any collaborator in my opinion. They were, nonetheless, powerful and influential within the jail system's inner workings. I reasoned that I might be able to use them to achieve my own goals.

I was aware that things were not going well for me. Because of my father, I was very sure they wouldn't torture or interrogate me, but I could see my uncle Ibrahim wasn't sure if I was telling the truth or not.

I wasn't sure either at the time.

I realised I'd been silly to believe the maj'd. Had I been as naive in trusting the Israelis? They had still not told me anything. They had not provided me with any contacts. Was that a game they were playing with me?

I went to my tent and found myself mentally and emotionally shutting down. I no longer had faith in anyone. Other inmates noticed something was amiss with me, but they had no idea what it was. Despite the fact that the maj'd kept what I told them to themselves, they never moved their gaze away from me. Everyone was sceptical of me. Similarly, I suspected everyone. And we all shared an open-air cage with nowhere else to go. There is nowhere to flee or hide.

Time flew by. Suspicion increased. Every day, there were screams, and every night, there was agony. Hamas tortured its own citizens! I simply couldn't excuse it, no matter how hard I tried.

It quickly deteriorated. Instead of just one person, three people would be investigated at the same time. At four o'clock in the morning, a man sprinted through the sector, scrambled up and over the outer fence, and was outside the camp in twenty seconds, his clothes and flesh ripped by the razor wire. A tower guard in Israel swung his machine gun around and took aim.

"Don't shoot!" yelled the man. "Don't fire! I'm not attempting to flee. I'm running away from them!" And he pointed to the panting maj'd peering through the fence at him. Soldiers burst through the gate, threw the convict to the ground, searched him, and removed him.

Was this the work of Hamas? Was this the religion of Islam?

Chapter 13: Riot

My father represented Islam to me.

If I were to weigh him on Allah's scale, he would be heavier than any other Muslim I had ever encountered. He never skipped a prayer. I regularly heard him praying and calling out to the god of the Qur'an in the middle of the night, even when he got home late and fatigued. He was humble, compassionate, and forgiving to my mother, his children, and even strangers.

My father was more than an apologist for Islam; he lived his life as an example of what a Muslim should be. He embodied the lovely side of Islam, not the harsh side that demanded its adherents conquer and subjugate the planet.

However, over the ten years that followed my incarceration, I witnessed him fight with an inner, inexplicable conflict. On the one hand, he did not consider the Muslims who murdered settlers, troops, and innocent women and children to be wrong. He believed Allah had given them the authority to do so. On the other hand, he was unable to perform what they did. Something in his soul turned it down. He rationalised what he couldn't justify as right for himself as right for others.

However, as a child, I only saw his virtues and imagined they were the result of his beliefs. Because I aspired to be like him, I accepted his beliefs without question. What I didn't realise at the time was that no matter how much we weighed on Allah's scale, our righteousness and good acts were worthless to God.

Nonetheless, the Muslims I encountered in Megiddo bore no similarity to my father. They assessed people as if they were superior to Allah himself. They were cruel and nasty, obstructing a television screen so we couldn't watch a bareheaded actress. They were racists and hypocrites, tormenting anyone who accumulated too many red points despite the fact that only the weakest and most vulnerable people appeared to accumulate these points. Prisoners with connections were granted immunity, including an admitted Israeli collaborator if he was the son of Sheikh Hassan Yousef.

For the first time in my life, I began to doubt things I had always believed in. "Eight twenty-three!"

It was finally time for my trial. I'd been in jail for six months. The IDF drove me to Jerusalem, where prosecutors requested that I be sentenced to sixteen months in prison.

At the very least, I got to see my family once a month. Every four weeks, my mother made the exhausting journey to Megiddo. She was only allowed to bring three of my brothers and sisters, so they alternated. And she always gave me a fresh batch of her delectable spinach burgers and baklava. My family never failed to pay us a visit.

Even though I couldn't tell them what was going on inside the fence and behind the curtains, seeing them was a huge comfort for me. Seeing me also seemed to alleviate some of their pain. I'd been like a father to my younger brothers and sisters, cooking for them, cleaning up after them, bathing and dressing them, and transporting them to and from school, and in prison I'd also become a resistance hero. They were quite proud of me.

During one of my visits, my mother informed me that my father had been released by the Palestinian Authority. I knew dad had always desired to perform hajj, or the pilgrimage to Mecca, and my mother reported he had left for Saudi Arabia soon after returning home. Hajj is the fifth pillar of Islam, and every Muslim who is physically and financially capable must perform it at least once in his or her lifetime. Every year, around two million people visit.

But my father never arrived. He was caught again when crossing the Allenby Bridge between Israel and Jordan, this time by Israelis.

* * *

One afternoon, the Hamas faction in Megiddo handed prison officials a list of petty requests, gave them 24 hours to meet them, and threatened rioting if they didn't.

Clearly, jail officials did not want an insurgency. A riot may result in convicts being shot, and Jerusalem's government bureaucrats didn't want to deal with the uproar that would ensue from the Red Cross and human rights organisations if that happened. Riots were a lose-lose situation for everyone involved. As a result, the Israelis encountered the major shaweesh, who was billeted in our section.

The only thing that kept running through my head was how absurd everything seemed. What are we doing? I was perplexed. This is insane! Because of that insane shaweesh? I wasn't a coward, but this was a waste of time. We were planning to throw tar chunks at the Israelis, who were well armed and shielded.

When Hamas gave the signal, prisoners in all sections began throwing wood, blacktop, and soap. A hundred black gas canisters soared into the sections and detonated within seconds, enveloping the camp with dense white fog. I couldn't make out anything. The stench was unbearable. Guys all around me collapsed to the ground, gasping for air.

All of this happened in three minutes. And the Israelis were only getting started.

Soldiers fired large pipes at us, spewing billows of yellow gas. But, unlike tear gas, it didn't float around in the air; instead, because it was heavier than air, it hugged the ground and pushed all the oxygen away. Inmates began to pass out.

When I saw the flames, I was trying to catch my breath.

The tent of Islamic Jihad in Quadrant Three was on fire. The flames surged twenty feet into the air in seconds. The tents were coated with a petroleum-based waterproofing then torched as if they had been saturated in gasoline. The wooden poles and frames, mattresses, and footlockers all caught fire. The wind spread the fire to the DFLP/PFLP and Fatah tents, and they were consumed by the blaze ten seconds later.

The blazing fire was heading straight toward us. A massive crackling tent fragment flew into the air and over the razor wire. Soldiers encircled us. There was just one way out: through the flames.

So we took off.

I quickly covered my face with a towel and dashed for the kitchen. The distance between the flaming tents and the wall was only ten feet. As the soldiers continued to flood the sector with yellow gas, more than 200 of us attempted to cross through at the same time.

Within minutes, half of Section Five had vanished, along with everything we possessed, of which there had been very little. Nothing but ashes remained.

Many inmates were injured. Fortunately, no one had been killed. Ambulances arrived to transport the injured, and those of us whose tents had burnt were relocated after the disturbances. I was relocated to the Hamas tent in Quadrant Two's centre.

The sole positive outcome of the Megiddo riots was the cessation of torture by Hamas officials. Surveillance persisted, but we felt more at ease and permitted ourselves to be less cautious. I made a couple of buddies that I believed I could trust. But mostly, I went about for hours by myself, day after day, doing nothing.

***

"Eight twenty-three!"

On September 1, 1997, a prison guard returned my stuff and the small amount of money I had with me when I was caught, shackled me, and escorted me to a van. The soldiers drove to Jenin in the West Bank, the first checkpoint they encountered in Palestinian territory. They opened the vehicle door and removed the handcuffs.

"You're free to go," replied one of the men. They then drove away in the opposite direction we had come from, leaving me alone on the side of the road.

It was impossible for me to believe. It felt great merely to step outside. I couldn't wait to see my mother and brothers and sisters. I was still two hours away from home, but I didn't want to walk fast. I wanted to enjoy my independence.

I walked for a few miles, filling my lungs with fresh air and my ears with soothing silence. I got a cab that brought me to the town centre as I began to feel more human. Another taxi transported me to Nablus, then to Ramallah, and finally to my house.

As I drove into Ramallah, seeing familiar shops and people, I yearned to get out of the taxi and immerse myself in it all. Before I got out of the taxi in front of my house, I noticed my mother standing at the doorway. As she shouted out to me, tears streamed down her cheeks. She dashed towards the car and wrapped her arms around me. All the grief she had been holding in for about a year and a half spilled out of her as she clutched to me and patted my back, shoulders, cheeks, and head.

"We've been counting the days until your return," she went on to say. "We were afraid we'd never see you again. Mosab, we are really proud of you. You truly are a hero."

I knew, like my father, that I couldn't tell her or my brothers and sisters what had happened to me. It would have been far too difficult for them. To them, I was a hero who had been imprisoned in Israel like the other heroes and was now returning home. They even considered it a positive experience for me, practically a rite of passage. Did my mother learn about guns? Yes. Did she think it was ridiculous? Possibly, but it all fell under the banner of resistance and was rationalised away.

We celebrated my return for the entire day, eating delicious food and laughing and having fun as we always did when we were together. It was almost as if I had never left. Many of my friends and my father's friends came to celebrate with us over the next few days.

I hung out at my mother's house for a few weeks, soaking up the love and gorging myself with her cuisine. Then I stepped outside and took in all the sights, sounds, and smells that I had missed so much. In the evenings, I spent time downtown with my friends, eating falafel at Mays Al Reem and drinking coffee at the Kit Kat with the shop's owner, Basam Huri. I inhaled the tranquillity and simplicity of freedom as I wandered the crowded streets and talked with my friends.

My mother had been pregnant again between my father's release from the PA prison and his re-arrest by the Israelis. My parents were taken aback because they had intended to cease having children after my sister Anhar was born seven years before. My mother was about six months pregnant when I arrived, and the baby was getting enormous. Then she broke her ankle, which took a long time to mend because our growing baby brother was devouring all of her calcium. We didn't have a wheelchair, so I had to carry her everywhere. She was in a lot of agony, and seeing her like that broke my heart. I acquired a driver's licence so we could go shopping and run errands. When Naser was born, I was in charge of feeding, washing, and changing his diapers. He began his life believing I was his father.

Needless to say, I failed my examinations and did not complete high school. The exam had been given to all of us in prison, but I was the only one who failed. I never understood why, because before the test, personnel from the Education Ministry came to the prison and handed out answer sheets to everyone. It was insane. One man, who was sixty years old and illiterate, had to have the answers written down for him. And he, too, passed! I had the answers as well, and I had been in school for twelve years, so I was familiar with the content. However, when the results came in, everyone passed except me. The only conclusion I could draw was that Allah did not want me to pass by cheating.

When I returned home, I enrolled in night classes at Al-Ahlia, a Catholic school in Ramallah. The majority of the pupils were devout Muslims who came because it was the greatest school in town. Going to school at night also allowed me to work during the day at the local Checkers hamburger joint to help support my family.

I only received a 64 percent on my examinations, but it was sufficient to pass. I hadn't worked hard because I wasn't very interested in the subject. I didn't mind. I was simply relieved to get that behind me.

Chapter 14: Damascus Road

My phone rang two months after I was released. "Congratulations," said an Arabic voice.

The accent was familiar to me. Loai, my "faithful" Shin Bet captain.

"We would love to see you," Loai added, "but we can't talk on the phone for long." "Can we get together?"

"Of course."

He provided me with a phone number, a password, and some instructions. I felt like a genuine spy. He urged me to go to one area, then another, and then phone him from there.

I followed his instructions, and when I called, I was given additional instructions. I walked for almost twenty minutes before a car parked beside me. I got into the car after a man inside instructed me to. I was searched, made to lie down on the floor, and blanketed.

We drove for approximately an hour without saying anything. We finally came to a halt inside a garage at someone's home. I was relieved it wasn't another military base or prison facility. Actually, it was a government-owned property in an Israeli settlement, as I later discovered. I was checked again as soon as I arrived, this time considerably more thoroughly, and escorted into a tastefully furnished living room. I waited there for a while until Loai entered. He shook my hand before hugging me.

"How are things going for you?" "How did you find your time in prison?"

I assured him I was alright and that my prison experience had not been pleasant, especially since he had told me I would only be there for a short period.

"I am sorry; we had to do that to protect you."

I reflected on my remarks to the maj'd about being a double agent and wondered if Loai was aware of them. I figured I should try to defend myself.

"Look," I explained, "they were torturing people inside, and I had no choice but to tell them I had agreed to work for you." I was terrified. You never informed me of what was going on inside. You never warned me I'd have to keep an eye out for my own folks. I was freaking out because you didn't train me. So I told them I agreed to be a collaborator in order to become a double agent and kill you guys."

Loai appeared astonished, but not angry. Though the Shin Bet could not condone torture within the prison, they were well aware of it and understood why I was terrified.

He contacted his boss and told him what I said. And, whether because it was so difficult for Israel to recruit Hamas members, or because I was a particularly attractive prize as the son of Sheikh Hassan Yousef, they let it go at that.

These Israelis were not at all what I had expected.

Loai handed me a few hundred dollars and urged me to go purchase some clothing for myself, take care of myself, and enjoy my life.

"We'll be in touch later," he promised.

What? Is there no covert mission? Is there no codebook? No gun? Just some cash and a hug? This made absolutely no sense.

We met up again a few weeks later, this time in a Shin Bet headquarters in the middle of Jerusalem. Every house was fully furnished, outfitted with alarms and guards, and so well hidden that not even the next-door neighbours knew what was going on inside.

The majority of the rooms were configured for meetings. And I was never permitted to leave one room without being escorted, not because they didn't trust me, but because they didn't want other Shin Bet agents to see me. Just another layer of protection.

Shin Bet members were exceedingly cordial during their second encounter. They were fluent in Arabic and clearly understood me, my family, and my culture. I had no information, and they demanded it. We merely discussed life in general.

This was not what I had anticipated. I genuinely wanted to know what they wanted me to do, but because of the files I'd read in prison, I was terrified they'd instruct me to do something stupid like have sex with my sister or neighbour and return them the tape. But nothing like that ever happened.

Loai gave me twice as much money after the second encounter as he did the first. I'd gotten approximately $800 from him in about a month, which was a lot of money for a twenty-year-old at the time. Despite this, I had offered the Shin Bet nothing in exchange. In truth, I learnt far more than I mentioned during my first several months as a Shin Bet agent.

My instruction began with some fundamental rules. I wasn't supposed to commit adultery because it would expose — or burn — me. In reality, I was advised not to have any unmarried relationships with women, Palestinian or Israeli, while working for them. I'd be gone if I did. And I wasn't supposed to tell anyone about my double-agent past.

Every time we met, I learnt something new about life, justice, and security. The Shin Bet was not attempting to break me down in order to force me to do horrible things. They appeared to be doing everything they could to help me grow, to make me stronger and smarter.

As time passed, I began to doubt my plan to kill the Israelis. These people were really nice. They obviously cared about me. Why would I wish to murder them? I was astonished to discover that I didn't.

The occupation had not ended. The Al-Bireh cemetery was still overflowing with the dead of Palestinian men, women, and children slain by Israeli soldiers. And I'd never forgotten the beating I'd received on the way to prison or the days I'd spent confined to that tiny chair.

But I also remembered the screams from the Megiddo torture tents and the man who nearly impaled himself on the razor-wire fence while fleeing his Hamas captors. Now I was gaining knowledge and insight. And who were my role models? My adversaries! But, in fact, were they? Or were they merely polite to me so they could take advantage of me? I was even more perplexed than I was before.

At one point in the conversation, Loai stated, "Since you are working with us, we are thinking about releasing your father so you can be close to him and see what is going on in the territories." I had no idea it was even a possibility, but I was relieved to have my father back.

My father and I would later swap notes on our experiences. He didn't like to go into detail about his ordeals, but he wanted me to know that he had made some amends during his time at Megiddo. He told me about a time when he was watching television in the mi'var and a board fell across the screen.

My uncle Ibrahim came to see me when my father was released from prison. My father also wanted him to know that he had put a halt to the torture in Megiddo and discovered that the vast majority of the men whose lives and families had been destroyed by the maj'd were innocent. Ibrahim pretended to be taken aback. When my father mentioned Akel, my uncle stated he tried to defend him and assured the maj'd Akel was not a collaborator.

It was impossible for me to believe. But that made perfect sense to the Israelis. My education, both in and out of the classroom, was an excellent investment for them. Working with someone who was uneducated and had no prospects would be risky for national security. It was also risky for me to be viewed as a loser, because the common knowledge on the streets of the territories was that only losers collaborated with the Israelis. This advice was obviously ill-conceived, because losers had nothing to offer the Shin Bet.

So I applied to Birzeit University, but they turned me down since my high school scores were inadequate. I mentioned that I had been in prison due to unique circumstances. I maintained that I was a bright young guy who would make an excellent student. They did not, however, make any exceptions. My only alternative was to attend Al-Quds Open University and study from home.

I did well in school this time. I was a little wiser and a lot more motivated than before. And who was I supposed to thank? My adversary.

"If you need anything, just let us know," my Shin Bet managers said whenever I met with them. You can go cleanse yourself. You are free to pray. You have nothing to be terrified of." They did not break Islamic law by providing me with food and water. My handlers were very careful not to do anything that would offend me: they didn't wear shorts. They didn't sit with their feet in my face and their legs on the desk. They were always courteous. As a result, I wanted to learn more from them. They didn't act like military robots. They were human beings, and they treated me as such. Every time we met, another stone fell from the basis of my worldview.

Not my father, but my culture, had taught me that the IDF and the Israeli people were my adversaries. My father didn't see soldiers; he saw individual persons carrying out their responsibilities as soldiers. His issue was not with people, but with the concepts that inspired and drove them.

Loai reminded me more of my father than any Palestinian I'd ever met. He didn't believe in Allah, yet he still respected me.

So who was my new adversary?

I discussed the torture in Megiddo with the Shin Bet. They claimed to know everything. Every movement of the captives, every word spoken, was recorded. They were aware of the hidden messages in dough balls, the torture tents, and the hole in the fence.

The world I knew was dissolving inexorably, revealing another universe that I was only now beginning to comprehend. Every time I met with the Shin Bet, I learnt something new about myself and others. If it wasn't indoctrination through mind-numbing repetition, famine, and sleep from the Israelis, perhaps other "infidels" could teach me something useful as well. After all, I wasn't fussy after hanging around with nominal Muslims, zealots, and atheists, the learned and the uneducated, right-wingers and left-wingers, Jews and Gentiles. And this gentleman appeared to be a simple man who invited me to come and talk rather than vote for Jesus in the next election.

"What do you think?" I inquired of Jamal. "Should we go?"

Jamal and I had been friends since we were children. We went to school, flung stones, and went to the mosque together. Jamal, who was six feet three and gorgeous, seldom said much. He rarely initiated a conversation, but he was an excellent listener. And we never argued, not even once.

We had grown up together and spent time in Megiddo Prison together. After Section Five burnt during the riots, Jamal was relocated alongside my cousin Yousef to Section Six and released from there.

Prison, however, had altered him. He stopped praying and going to the mosque, and he started smoking. He was gloomy and spent most of his time at home watching television. At the very least, I had ideals to hang onto while in prison. But because Jamal came from a secular household that did not follow Islam, his faith was too frail to keep him together.

Jamal stared at me, and I could see he was eager to attend the Bible study. He was plainly as intrigued—and bored—as I was. But something inside him fought back.

I knew Jamal meant well, but I wasn't concerned. My father had always encouraged us to be open-minded and caring toward everyone, including those who did not share our beliefs. I lowered my gaze to the Bible in my lap.

My father possessed a massive library of 5,000 books, including a Bible. I had read the sexual parts in the Song of Solomon as a child, but I never went any further. This New Testament, on the other hand, was a gift. Because presents are cherished and respected in Arab culture, I concluded that reading it was the least I could do.

I started at the beginning, and by the time I came to the Sermon on the Mount, I was thinking, Wow, this Jesus man is very great! Everything he says is lovely. I couldn't put down the book. Every verse seemed to hit a raw nerve in my life. It was a simple statement, yet it had the ability to heal my soul and offer me hope.

Then I read, "You've heard it said, 'Love your neighbour and hate your enemy.'" But I tell you, love your enemies and pray for those who persecute you, so that you may be called sons of God" (Matthew 5:43-45).

That's all! These remarks shook me to my core. I'd never heard anything like that before, but I knew it was the message I'd been looking for my entire life.

For years, I struggled to identify my adversary, and I looked for foes outside of Islam and Palestine. But then I realised that the Israelis were not my adversaries. Neither was it Hamas, my uncle Ibrahim, the boy who hit me with the butt of his M16, or the apelike detention centre guard. I observed that opponents were not characterised by their nationality, religion, or skin colour. I realised that we all have the same common enemies: greed, pride, and all the horrible thoughts and devilish shadows that exist within us.

That meant I could fall in love with anyone. The only true adversary was the one within me.

Five years ago, I would have read Jesus' statements and said, What an idiot!, and discarded the Bible. But my encounters with my mad butcher neighbour, the family members and religious authorities who abused me while my father was in prison, and my own time at Megiddo had all prepared me for the intensity and beauty of this reality. Wow! was all I could say in response. What insight this man possessed!

"Do not judge, or you will be judged," Jesus stated (Matthew 7:1). What a contrast between him and Allah! Islam's god was harsh, and Arab culture followed Allah's example.

When Jesus criticised the hypocrisy of the scribes and Pharisees, I remembered my uncle. I remembered him being upset when he was invited to a prestigious event and not being given the best seat in the house. It was as if Jesus was speaking directly to Ibrahim and every sheikh and imam in Islam.

Everything Jesus said in this book made complete sense to me. I began to cry because I was so overwhelmed.

God used the Shin Bet to teach me that Israel was not my enemy, and now he has placed the answers to the rest of my questions in my hands in the form of a small New Testament. But I still had a long way to go in terms of knowing the Bible. Muslims are taught to accept all of God's books, including the Torah and the Bible. However, we are taught that men have modified the Bible, rendering it untrustworthy. Mohammad said that the Qur'an was God's last and inerrant word to men. So I'd have to relinquish my notion that the Bible had been changed first. Then I'd have to figure out how to make both books function in my life, how to integrate Islam and Christianity. Reconciling the irreconcilable is no easy task.

At the same time, while I believed in Jesus' teachings, I did not associate him with being God. Nonetheless, my standards had shifted abruptly and profoundly as a result of being inspired by the Bible rather than the Qur'an.

I kept reading my New Testament and going to Bible study. I went to church and said to myself, "This is not the religious Christianity I see in Ramallah." This is true. The Christians I had previously known were no different than orthodox Muslims. They professed to be religious, but they didn't practise it.

I started spending more time with people from the Bible study and discovered that I truly like their company. We had so much fun talking about our lives, our backgrounds, and our views. They were always respectful of my Muslim ancestry and culture. And I discovered that when I was among them, I could truly be myself.

I yearned to incorporate what I was learning into my own culture, realising that the occupation was not to blame for our plight. Our challenge was far more complex than military and politics.

I wondered what Palestinians would do if Israel vanished—if everything not only returned to the way it was before 1948, but if all Jews abandoned the Holy Land and were scattered once more. And I knew the answer for the first time.

We'd still fight. For nothing. Over a female who isn't wearing a headscarf. Over who was the most difficult and crucial. Over who gets to write the rules and who gets the finest seat.

It was the year 1999. I was twenty-one years old at the time. My life was changing, and the more I learnt, the more perplexed I got.

"God, the Creator, please show me the truth," I pleaded every day. "I'm perplexed. I'm at a loss. And I'm not sure which way to go."

Chapter 15: Second Intifada

Hamas, formerly the Palestinians' dominant force, was in ruins. The broken organisation's bitter opponent for hearts and minds was now fully in charge.

The Palestinian Authority had done what Israel had been unable to do via mere force through intrigue and deal making. It had eliminated Hamas' military wing and imprisoned its commanders and members. Even after their release, Hamas militants returned home and did nothing more to oppose the PA or the occupation. The young fedayeen were completely fatigued. Their leaders were split and distrustful of one another.

My father was again on his own, so he returned to working at the mosque and refugee camps. When he spoke now, he did it in the name of Allah, not as Hamas' leader. I appreciated the opportunity to travel and spend time with him again after years of separation due to our various imprisonments. I had missed our lengthy discussions about life and Islam.

As I began to read my Bible and learn about Christianity, I found myself captivated by the grace, love, and humility that Jesus spoke of. Surprisingly, it was those same qualities that drew people to my father—one of the most devout Muslims I had ever met.

Concerning my relationship with the Shin Bet, there seemed to be nothing for me to do now that Hamas was mostly out of the picture and the PA was keeping things calm. We were no longer strangers. They could let me leave whenever they wanted, or I could say goodbye whenever I chose.

* * *

On the evening of September 27, my father knocked on my door and asked if I would drive him to Marwan Barghouti's residence after dawn prayer the next morning.

Marwan Barghouti was the secretary-general of Fatah, the PLO's largest political faction. He was a prominent young Palestinian politician who was a staunch supporter of a Palestinian state and a critic of the PA's and Arafat's security forces' corruption and human rights violations. Marwan, a short, laid-back man who generally wore blue jeans, was widely expected to be the next Palestinian president.

"What's going on?" I inquired of my father.

"Sharon is scheduled to visit the Al-Aqsa Mosque tomorrow, and the PA believes this is a good opportunity to launch an uprising."

Ariel Sharon was the leader of the conservative Likud Party and Prime Minister Ehud Barak's left-leaning Labor Party. Sharon was in the midst of a political battle with Barak for the leadership of the Israeli government.

An insurgency? Were they for real? The PA leaders who had imprisoned my father were now encouraging him to assist organise another intifada. It was infuriating, but it wasn't difficult to figure out why they approached my father about this plan. They knew the people liked and trusted him just as much as they despised and distrusted the PA. They would follow my father anywhere, and the leadership was well aware of this.

They also knew that Hamas, like a beaten boxer, was out for the count. They wanted my father to pick it up, spray it with water, and send it in for another round so the PA could knock it out in front of a cheering crowd. Even Hamas leaders, tired from years of violence, cautioned my father to be cautious.

But my father saw the significance of this gesture. If he did not appear to be cooperating with the PA, they would simply blame

Hamas for destabilising the peace process.

Whatever we did, we appeared to be in a lose-lose situation, and I was quite concerned about the idea. But I knew my father had to do it, so I drove him to Marwan Barghouti's house the next morning. We knocked, had no quick response, and soon discovered that Marwan was still in bed.

Typical, I thought to myself. Fatah includes my father in their idiotic ideas and then refuses to get out of bed to help carry them out.

"Never mind," I explained to my father. "Don't even bother. "Get in your car, and I'll drive you to Jerusalem."

Of course, driving my father to Sharon's visit location was dangerous, given that most Palestinian cars were not permitted to enter Jerusalem. Ordinarily, if an Israeli police officer caught a Palestinian motorist, he would be penalised, but considering who we were, my father and I would almost certainly be jailed on the scene. I had to be extremely cautious, staying on side roads and trusting that my Shin Bet contacts would protect me if necessary.

My father and I arrived at the location just a few minutes before Sharon. It was a peaceful morning. A hundred Palestinians had gathered to worship. Sharon arrived during typical tourist hours, accompanied by a Likud delegation and almost a thousand riot police. He came in, took a look around, and then departed. He didn't say anything. He never went inside the mosque.

The Ramallah demonstration was far from a dramatic display of spontaneous combustion. It was still early in the morning, and people were going about their daily lives, wondering what was up with these students and Hamas members who didn't appear to grasp what they were protesting.

A handful of males stood up with bullhorns and made statements, while the small group of Palestinians gathered around them occasionally chanted and shouted in response. But, for the most part, no one seemed to care all that much. Within the Palestinian territory, things had cooled down considerably. Every day was just another day at work. Israeli soldiers had become a permanent feature. Palestinians were permitted to work and attend school within Israel. Ramallah had a vibrant nightlife, so it was tough to figure out what these guys were so excited about.

This demonstration appeared to be another non-event in my opinion. So I phoned some Bible study pals and we drove up to Galilee to camp near the lake.

I was cut off from all news sources, so I had no idea that the next morning, a huge number of rock-throwing Palestinian activists clashed with Israeli riot police near the site of Sharon's visit. The rock tossing progressed to the use of Molotov cocktails, followed by firing with Kalashnikovs. To disperse the protests, police deployed rubber-coated metal bullets and, according to some sources, live ammunition. Four demonstrators were murdered, and over 200 more were injured. Fourteen police officers were also hurt. And all of this was exactly what the Palestinian Authority had predicted.

Yasser Arafat and the other Palestinian Authority leaders were dead set on starting another intifada. They had been planning it for months, even while Arafat and Barak were in Camp David with President Clinton. They had only been waiting for the right pretext. Sharon's visit presented precisely such an opportunity. So, after a few false starts, the Al-Aqsa Intifada began in earnest, rekindling the tinderbox of passions in the West Bank and Gaza. Particularly in Gaza.

There, Fatah started demonstrations that resulted in the death of a twelve-year-old child called Mohammed al-Dura, which was broadcast worldwide. The youngster and his father, Jamal, had become trapped in the crossfire and sought refuge behind a concrete cylinder. A stray gunshot struck the boy, who died in his father's arms. A Palestinian cameraman working for French public television filmed the entire heartbreaking scene. Within hours, the video clip had gone viral, enraging millions against Israel's occupation.

However, this episode would spark a heated international debate in the months that followed. Some pointed to evidence that Palestinian shooting was to blame for the boy's death. Others continued to point the finger at the Israelis. Some even claimed that the clip was a well orchestrated fraud. Many suspected a PLO propaganda tactic because the tape did not show the youngster being shot or even his body. If this was the case, it was smart and efficient.

Whatever the truth was, I found myself in the midst of a conflict in which my father was a significant commander—albeit a leader who had no idea what he was leading or where it would lead him. Arafat and Fatah were merely using and using him to stir up trouble, presenting the PA with new bargaining chips and fund-raising fodder.

Meanwhile, people were dying at the checkpoints once more. Every side was shooting indiscriminately. Children were being slaughtered. Day after deadly day, a weeping Yasser Arafat stood in front of Western TV cameras, wringing his hands and denying any involvement in the carnage. Instead, he pointed the accusation at my father, Marwan Barghouti, and the refugees in the camps. He informed the world that he was doing all possible to quell the rebellion. But his other finger was solidly on the trigger the entire time.

However, Arafat soon learned that he had unleashed a horrible genie. He had jolted the Palestinians awake and roused them because it served his purposes. But it didn't take long for them to spiral out of control. People grew so outraged after seeing IDF soldiers shoot down their dads, mothers, and children that they refused to listen to the PA or anybody else.

Arafat also realised that the battered boxer he had resurrected was tougher than he had thought. The streets were Hamas' natural environment. The boxer got its start there, and it was at its most powerful there.

Is there going to be peace with Israel? What about Camp David? Oslo? What about half of Jerusalem? Forget it all! In the white-hot furnace of contention, any desire for compromise had vanished. Palestinians had reverted to their old all-or-nothing mentality. And now it was Hamas, not Arafat, who was fueling the fires.

What I was seeing was unbelievable. Something has to be done to put a stop to this lunacy. I knew it was time for me to start working with Shin Bet. And I threw myself into it wholeheartedly.

Chapter 16: Undercover

Except for a few members of Israeli intelligence, what I am about to reveal is unknown to the rest of the world. I'm sharing this knowledge in the hope that it will shed light on some major events that have long been cloaked in obscurity.

On the day of decision—the day I resolved to do everything in my power to put an end to the madness—I began by researching everything I could about Marwan Barghouti and the Hamas leaders' activities and ambitions. I informed the Shin Bet, which was doing everything it could to find these leaders.

I was given the code name the Green Prince by the Shin Bet. Green was the colour of the Hamas flag, and prince was an apparent reference to my father's role as a king inside Hamas. As a result, at the age of twenty-two, I became the Shin Bet's sole Hamas insider capable of infiltrating Hamas' military and political wings, as well as other Palestinian factions.

But this was not solely my duty. It was evident to me by this point that God had purposefully placed me at the heart of Hamas and Palestinian leadership, in Yasser Arafat's meetings, and with the Israeli security service. I was in a rare position to do the task. And I had the impression that God was with me.

I wanted to delve deep, to understand all that was going on. I had been in the thick of the First Intifada, surrounded by death and destruction. The dead had overrun a cemetery where I had played soccer as a child. I flung rocks. I broke curfew. But I couldn't understand why our people were so violent. Now I was curious as to why we were doing it all over again. I needed to comprehend.

According to Yasser Arafat, the rebellion was all about politics, money, and retaining power. He was the Palestinian puppet master, a skillful manipulator. On video, he criticised Hamas for its attacks on Israeli people. He stressed that Hamas does not represent the PA or the Palestinian people. But he did little to intervene, preferring to let Hamas do his dirty job while the international world took the heat. He had evolved into a cunning elderly politician who understood that Israel could not halt the attacks without collaborating with the Palestinian Authority. And the more strikes there were, the sooner Israel would agree to a deal.

A new group arrived on the scene around this time. It was known as the Al-Aqsa Martyrs Brigades. Its preferred targets were IDF soldiers and settlers. However, no one knew who these men were or where they came from. They appeared religious, despite the fact that neither Hamas nor Islamic Jihad knew them. They did not appear to be nationalist offshoots of the Palestinian Authority or Fatah.

Everyone, including the Shin Bet, was perplexed. Every once in a while, another settler's automobile or bus was hit with lethal precision. Even heavily armed Israeli forces couldn't stop this bunch.

I travelled through central Ramallah that evening. The streets were deserted because it was Ramadan. As I arrived into a parking lot down the road from Maher Odeh's apartment complex, the sun had fallen and everyone was breaking their daily fast. Despite the fact that I hadn't been trained for this type of job, I knew the fundamentals. In the movies, men sit in a car across the street from the suspect's house, monitoring him with expensive cameras and other espionage equipment. Despite the Shin Bet's access to advanced equipment, the only tools I had for this job were my automobile and my eyes. I only needed to keep an eye on the building and keep note of who arrived and went.

After around 30 minutes, several armed guys exited the two-story building and entered a new green Chevy with Israeli licence plates. The entire scene was incorrect. To begin with, Hamas members, particularly those from the military branch, never carried weapons in public. Second, persons like Maher Odeh did not associate with armed men. I started my car and waited for a few cars to pass in front of us before pulling out. I followed the green Chevy along the main street toward Betunia, where my folks resided, and suddenly I lost sight of them.

I was furious at both myself and the Shin Bet. This was nothing like you'd seen in the movies. This was real life, and snooping could get you killed in real life. They needed to send me some support if they wanted me to follow armed individuals like that, especially at night. This was a team effort, not a solo effort. I had always believed that a mission like this would include air and satellite surveillance—fancy high-tech stuff. But it was just me. I may have been lucky, or I could have been shot. In this scenario, I received nothing. I drove home feeling like a businessman who had just lost a million-dollar sale.

I got up the next morning, determined to find that car. But after hours of driving, I came up empty. I gave up, frustrated once more, and went to wash my car. And there it was, right inside the car wash. The same green Chevrolet. The same folks. The same weapons.

Was this luck, God's intervention, or something else?

I could see them better now that it was morning, and I was closer to them than I had been the night before. I identified them right away as Force 17, an elite commando force that had been around since the early 1970s, with their beautiful clothes, AK-47s, and M16s. These were the men who kept an eye on Arafat and defended him from an increasing list of aspirants and usurpers.

Something didn't feel quite right. They couldn't be the same men I saw at Maher Odeh, could they? What would Maher Odeh do with a gunman? He had nothing to do with Arafat, did he? Nothing made any sense.

I questioned the owner of the car wash who they were after they left. He knew I was Hassan Yousef's son, so my questions came as no surprise to him. He acknowledged they were from Force 17 and said they lived in Betunia. Now I was even more perplexed. Why did these guys choose to live a few minutes away from my parents' house rather than in Arafat's compound?

I arrived at the address I had received from the car-wash proprietor and discovered the Chevy parked outside. I dashed straight to Shin Bet headquarters and informed Loai of my findings. He was attentive, but his boss continued to argue with me.

He was furious that I had spoken to him in that manner and rushed out of the meeting. Loai encouraged me to calm down and go over all of the details again. The Chevy, it seems, did not fit the information they knew on the Brigades. It was a stolen Israeli car, which was typical of PA personnel, but we couldn't figure out how it linked them to the new faction.

I was certain it was a green Chevy, but I returned to my apartment regardless. The Chevy was still parked in the same position. However, outside the apartment, I noticed another car covered in a white sheet. I snuck up to the building's side and carefully lifted the sheep's back corner. A 1982 silver BMW sat beneath.

He went on to say that this material was a genuine breakthrough since it was the first proof that the Al-Aqsa Martyrs Brigades were Yasser Arafat's own guards, sponsored directly by him using American and international taxpayer money. Finding this link was a crucial step in putting an end to the awful spate of explosions that were killing innocent victims. The proof I provided to the Shin Bet would subsequently be used against Arafat in front of the United Nations Security Council. All we had to do now was apprehend the members of this new cell, or, as the Israelis put it, "cut off the head of the snake."

We discovered that the most dangerous members were Brigades head Ahmad Ghandour and one of his lieutenants Muhaned Abu Halawa. They'd already murdered a dozen individuals. It didn't appear to be a tough chore to put these individuals out of business. We were aware of who they were and where they lived. And, most importantly, they had no idea we knew.

The IDF sent an unmanned drone to gather intelligence from the apartment complex. Two days later, the Brigades launched another strike inside Israel, prompting the Israelis to respond. A sixty-five-ton Israeli Merkava battle tank's 120 mm weapon fired twenty shells into the Brigades' building. Unfortunately, no one had checked the surveillance drone to determine if the guys were still present. They didn't.

Worse, they now knew we were watching them. They sought safety, predictably, in Yasser Arafat's compound. We knew they were there, but it was politically impossible to go in and rescue them at the time. Their attacks were becoming more regular and vicious.

Ahmad Ghandour was at the top of the wanted list because he was a leader. We thought we'd never catch him after he moved inside the compound. We didn't, as it turned out. He obtained himself.

I happened upon a military funeral while walking down the street near Al-Bireh's old cemetery one day.

* * *

I accompanied my father wherever he went during the first years of the Al-Aqsa Intifada. I was his protégé, bodyguard, confidant, learner, and friend as his firstborn son. And he was everything to me—my model of what it meant to be a guy. Though our ideas were clearly no longer compatible, I knew his heart was in the right place and his intentions were good. His love for Muslims and commitment to Allah never wavered. He yearned for peace among his people and had dedicated his life to achieving it.

This second revolt was mostly a West Bank phenomenon. There had been a few protests in Gaza, and the death of the young Mohammed al-Dura had fanned the flames. But it was Hamas that fanned the flames in the West Bank.

Angry crowds clashed with Israeli soldiers in every village, town, and city. Every checkpoint turned into a bloodbath. It was difficult to discover someone who had not recently buried close friends or family members.

Meanwhile, top-level, high-profile men from all Palestinian groups met regularly with Yasser Arafat to coordinate their operations. My father represented Hamas, which had once again grown to be the largest and most powerful group. Apart from the others, he, Marwan Barghouti, and Arafat met weekly. I was permitted to join my father to those intimate sessions multiple times.

I detested Arafat and what he was doing to people I cared about. But, given my status as a Shin Bet mole, it was absolutely inappropriate for me to express my emotions. Nonetheless, after Arafat kissed me, I quickly wiped my cheek. He was definitely embarrassed when he noticed. My father was humiliated. That was the last time my father took me with him.

The intifada leaders always arrived for those daily meetings in their seven-thousand-dollar foreign cars, accompanied by additional cars full of bodyguards. My father, on the other hand, always drove in his dark blue 1987 Audi. There was no bodyguard, just myself.

These gatherings were the intifada's driving force. Even though I had to sit outside the conference room, I knew everything that happened inside since my father took notes. I had access to those notes and copied them. The notes never contained any highly sensitive information, such as the who, where, and when of a military action.

Rather, the leaders always spoke in broad strokes that revealed patterns and intentions, such as centering an attack on Israel or targeting settlers or checkpoints.

The conference notes did, however, give demonstration dates. If my father announced that Hamas will hold a rally tomorrow at one o'clock in the centre of Ramallah, runners would be dispatched to mosques, refugee camps, and schools to notify all Hamas members to be present at one o'clock. Israeli forces also arrived. As a result, Muslims, refugees, and, far too frequently, schoolchildren have been slaughtered.

The truth is that Hamas was all but extinct before the Second Intifada. My father should have ignored it. Every day, the Arab world saw his face and heard his voice on Al-Jazeera TV. He was now the intifada's visible leader. That made him extremely famous and influential throughout the Muslim world, but it also made him the ultimate evil man in Israel's eyes.

Hassan Yousef, on the other hand, was not puffed up at the conclusion of the day. He was merely humbly satisfied that he had done Allah's will.

One morning, while reading my father's meeting notes, I noticed that a demonstration had been planned. The next day, I followed him at the front of the roaring mob to an Israeli checkpoint. The leaders split out and moved to the safety of a hilltop two hundred yards before we reached the checkpoint. Everyone else—young men and children from the schools—rushed forward and began throwing stones at the heavily armed soldiers, who fired into the mob in response.

Even rubber-coated bullets could be lethal in these scenarios. Children were especially vulnerable. When fired at a range closer than the minimum forty metres specified by IDF standards, this ammunition proved easily fatal.

We could see dead and wounded people everywhere from our vantage point on the hill. Soldiers even opened fire on arriving ambulances, firing at drivers and killing those trying to help the injured. It was excruciating.

Everyone was soon shooting. The checkpoint was pelted with stones. Thousands pushed against the walls, attempting to force their way past the soldiers, driven by a single desire, a single thought: to reach Beit El and destroy everything and everyone in their path. They were mad, enraged by the sight of dead loved ones and the smell of blood.

When it appeared that things couldn't be much more chaotic, a Merkava's 1200 horsepower diesel engine roared into the melee. Its gun shattered the air with a sonic boom.

The tank was responding to PA fighters who had begun firing at IDF soldiers. Bodyguards grabbed their charges and whisked them away as the tank advanced. As I attempted to bring my father to the car, chunks of bodies covered the hill beneath our feet. When we finally arrived, we dashed into Ramallah, heading for the hospital, which was teeming with the injured, dying, and dead. There were insufficient rooms. The Red Crescent set up shop outside in a last-ditch effort to keep individuals from bleeding to death before they could get in. But that was simply insufficient.

The blood was spread on the hospital's walls and flooring. People slipped on it as they walked along the halls. Husbands and fathers, wives and mothers, and children wept and wailed in agony.

Surprisingly, in the middle of their grief and anger, the people appeared to be tremendously grateful for the Palestinian leaders, such as my father, who had come to share their grief and anger with them. Yet these were the same Palestinian officials who had herded them and their children like goats to the slaughter before ducking out of the way to watch the carnage from a safe distance. That made me sicker than the gore.

That was just one demonstration. We sat in front of the television night after night, listening to the never-ending litany of the dead. This city has ten. There are five of them. Here are twenty more.

I read one report of a man named Shada who was drilling a hole in the wall of a building across from a protest. When an Israeli tank gunner noticed him, he mistook the drill for a cannon. He fired a cannon shell at Shada's head.

My father and I went to the house of the slain man. He had a lovely new bride. However, that was not the worst of it. The Palestinian officials who had come to console the widow began squabbling over who would preach at Shada's funeral. For three days, who would be in charge of receiving mourners? Who would be in charge of the family's food? They were all calling Shada "our son," claiming that he was a member of their side and proving that their faction was more involved in the intifada than the others.

The rival factions had devolved into absurd arguing over the dead. And, for the most part, the dead were people who had nothing to do with the movement. They were just ordinary people caught up in a wave of emotion. Many others, like Shada, simply happened to be in the wrong place at the wrong time. While this was going on, Arabs around the world were burning American and Israeli flags, protesting, and pouring billions of money into Palestinian lands to end the occupation. Saddam Hussein donated thirty-five million dollars to the families of Palestinian martyrs during the first two and a half years of the Second Intifada—ten thousand dollars to the family of anybody murdered fighting Israel and twenty-five thousand dollars to the family of every suicide bomber. A lot could be said about this pointless struggle over real estate. But you could never call life cheap.

Chapter 17: Most Wanted

Palestinians no longer held Yasser Arafat or Hamas responsible for their problems. They now blame Israel for the deaths of their children. But I couldn't help but wonder: Why were those children out there in the first place? Where had the parents gone? Why didn't their mothers and fathers confine them? Those children should have been at school, not running around the streets throwing stones at armed soldiers.

In the midst of all of this, and especially with large sums of money arriving from Iraq's cruel ruler, Saddam Hussein, Hamas discovered that it had lost its monopoly on suicide bombing. The bombers now included members of Islamic Jihad and the Al-Aqsa Martyrs Brigades, as well as secularists, communists, and atheists. And they were all competing to see who could kill the most Israeli citizens.

There was an excessive amount of blood. I couldn't fall asleep. I couldn't eat anything. I no longer saw it solely through the perspective of a Muslim, a Palestinian, or even the son of Hassan Yousef. Now I see everything through Israeli eyes as well. Even more crucially, I witnessed the senseless massacre through the eyes of Jesus, who wept for those who perished. The more I read the Bible, the clearer one single fact became to me: loving and forgiving one's adversaries is the only true method to put an end to the slaughter.

But, as much as I admired Jesus, I didn't believe my Christian friends when they said he was God. My god was Allah. But, whether I realised it or not, I was progressively adopting Jesus' values and rejecting Allah's. The hypocrisy I saw all around me hastened my departure from Islam. According to Islam, a committed servant of Allah who died as a martyr went immediately to heaven. There will be no strange angels interrogating you or tormenting the dead. But, all of a sudden, anyone killed by Israelis—whether a nominal

Muslim, a communist, or even an atheist—appeared to be a holy martyr. The imams and sheikhs informed the bereaved families, "Your loved one is in heaven."

Of course, the Qur'an contradicted their claims. Who goes to heaven and who goes to hell is clearly stated in the Qur'an. However, these leaders did not appear to care. This wasn't even about truth or theology; it was about deceiving people for strategic and political gain. It was about Islamic leaders drugging their people with lies in order to distract them from the misery those leaders were inflicting on them.

As the Shin Bet passed on more and more material to me, I was constantly astounded by what they knew about the people in my life—often former friends who had turned out to be quite dangerous characters. Some have even joined the hard core of Hamas' armed branch. Daya Muhammad Hussein Al-Tawil was one of them. His uncle was a Hamas leader, and he was a lovely young man.

Daya had never been religious in all the years I had known him. Actually, his father was a communist, thus he had nothing to do with Islam. His mother was a Muslim in the cultural sense, but she was far from extremist. And his sister was a journalist educated in the United States, a U.S. citizen, and a modern woman who did not wear a headscarf. They were all well educated and lived in a comfortable home. Daya had graduated top in his class from Birzeit University's engineering program. He had never attended a Hamas demonstration, to the best of my knowledge.

Given all of this, I was astonished to learn that Daya had blown himself up near the French Hill crossroads in Jerusalem on March 27, 2001. Despite the fact that no one else was killed, twenty-nine Israelis were injured.

Daya wasn't a dumb kid who could be easily persuaded to do

anything like this. He wasn't a destitute refugee with nothing to lose. He didn't require money. So, what drove him to do it? Nobody could understand. His parents, like me, were taken aback. Even Israel's intelligence services were baffled.

Muhammad Jamal al-Natsheh, who helped form Hamas with my father and eventually became the leader of its military arm in the West Bank, was the prime suspect. Al-Natsheh was from the most powerful family in the region, thus he had nothing to fear. He stood about six feet tall and was built like a warrior—tough, muscular, and intellectual. Despite his hatred for Jews, I knew him to be a really loving individual.

Another person on the list was Saleh Talahme, an electrical engineer who was exceptionally smart and well educated. I had no idea at the time, but the two of us would become extremely close friends.

Ibrahim Hamed oversaw the security wing in the West Bank. Sayyed al-Sheikh Qassem and Hasaneen Rummanah aided these three men.

* * *

Maybe my life wasn't complicated enough, or maybe it just seemed like a good idea at the time, but I started working in the Capacity-Building Office of the United States Agency for International Development (USAID) Village Water and Sanitation Program, which is headquartered in Al-Bireh, the same month.

I know it's a long title, but it was a really important project. I started as a receptionist because I didn't have a college degree.

Some of the Christians I went to Bible study with had connected me to one of the American managers, who liked me right away and gave me a position. Loai thought it would make an excellent cover because my new US Embassy-stamped ID card would allow me to easily move between Israel and the Palestinian territories. It would also keep folks from being suspicious about why I always had a lot of money to spend.

Water has long been a contentious topic in the Bible's homeland. For modern Israel, the dynamic has shifted along with the country's borders. For example, one of the results of the 1967 Six-Day War was Israel gaining control of the Golan Heights from Syria. This effectively handed Israel control of the entire Sea of Galilee, as well as the Jordan River and every other spring and torrent that flowed into and out of it. In violation of international law, Israel diverted water from the Jordan River away from the West Bank and Gaza Strip via its National Water Carrier, supplying Israeli citizens and settlers with over three-quarters of the water from West Bank aquifers. The US has spent hundreds of millions of dollars drilling wells and building independent water sources for my people.

USAID was more than just a front for me. The people that worked there became my pals. I knew God had given me this position. It was policy at USAID not to hire anyone who was politically involved, let alone someone whose father was the leader of a major terrorist organisation.

But my supervisor opted to keep me for whatever reason. His generosity would soon pay off in ways he had no idea about.

Because of the intifada, the US government permitted its personnel to access the West Bank only for the purpose of working. However, this required them to pass through perilous checkpoints. They would have been safer living in the West Bank than going through checkpoints every day and driving about in 4 × 4 American jeeps with yellow Israeli tags. The average Palestinian couldn't tell the difference between those who came to help and those who came to kill.

Loai warned me not long after I started working for USAID that security personnel would be arriving in Ramallah the next day. I cautioned my American manager not to come to town and told everyone else to stay at home. I told him I couldn't tell him how I received this knowledge, but I pushed him to believe me. He did. He presumably assumed I had inside information because I was Hassan Yousef's son.

The following day, Ramallah was on fire. People were racing through the streets, firing at anything and everything they saw. Cars were set on fire on the side of the road, and shop windows were smashed, leaving the establishments susceptible to thieves and looters. When my supervisor heard the news, he told me, "Please, Mosab, let me know whenever something like that happens again."

"OK," I said, "but only if you don't ask any questions." If I tell you not to come, don't come."

Chapter 18: Torn

On August 9, 2001, just before 2 p.m., twenty-two-year-old Izz al-Din Shuheil al-Masri blew himself up inside the busy Sbarro pizza eatery on King George Street and Jaffa Road. Al-Masri came from a wealthy family in the West Bank.

Five to 10 kg of explosives rained nails, nuts, and bolts into the summer crowd, killing 15 and injuring 130. Between this atrocity and the Dolphinarium explosion a few months earlier, Israelis were practically blinded by grief and hatred. Whatever gang or faction was responsible for these atrocities needed to be discovered and stopped before more innocent people died. Otherwise, events would very certainly escalate out of control, causing tremendous death and heartbreak across the region. The Shin Bet investigated every detail of the bombing, attempting to link it to the five men at the safe house—Muhammad Jamal al-Natsheh, Saleh Talahme, Ibrahim Hamed, Sayyed al-Sheikh Qassem, and Hasaneen Rummanah—but there was no evidence linking them to the Dolphinarium or Sbarro attacks.

Who could have created such weapons? Certainly not a student of chemistry or engineering. We knew everything about them, from their grades to what they ate for breakfast.

Whoever was making these explosives was an expert, didn't appear to be associated with any of the Palestinian factions, and was operating well below the radar of the Israelis. We have to find him before he constructs any more bombs. This person was quite dangerous.

Halawa was a Fatah field commander who served with Force 17. Discipline, skill, and keen training come to mind when thinking of elite warriors like Force 17 and Saddam Hussein's Republican Guards. However, Halawa did not fit the model. He was an illiterate loose cannon who frequently carried one of the massive machine guns that were commonly placed on jeeps. Halawa often gave guns to other extremists and unsavoury personalities, who subsequently utilised them when driving by checkpoints, indiscriminately strafing soldiers and bystanders.

In May, for example, he gave someone two loaded AK-47s and a sack of bullets. Not long after, this man and a companion ambushed a Greek Orthodox monk named Tsibouktsakis Germanus on a route leading out of Jerusalem and fired thirteen of those bullets into him. Halawa rewarded the murders with extra weapons in preparation for an attack on Hebrew University on Mount Scopus.

It wasn't long before Israel placed pressure on the Shin Bet to permanently shut down Halawa. I was the sole Shin Bet agent who could identify him because of my Hamas ties. But, for the first time in my life, I was confronted with a genuine moral quandary. Something inside of me was vehemently opposed to killing this man, no matter how horrible he was.

I went home and took out my well-worn Bible. I looked and looked and couldn't find anything in the Bible that would justify murder. But I couldn't bear the thought of the blood on my hands if we allowed him to keep alive and shoot people. I felt trapped.

I continued to contemplate and pray to God Almighty until I eventually said, "Forgive me, Lord, for what I am about to do." Please forgive me. This dude is doomed.

"That's good," Loai responded after hearing my decision. "We'll find him. You just need to make sure Marwan Barghouti isn't in the car with him."

Marwan was not simply a powerful Palestinian, but also a terrorist with a long history of killing Israelis. Even though the Shin Bet despised him, they did not want him killed since he would make a formidable martyr.

I was sitting in my car outside of Barghouti's office on August 4, 2001, when I noticed Halawa walk in. He emerged a few hours later, got into his gold VW Golf, and drove away. I called the police and assured them that Halawa was safe.

IDF troops monitored Halawa's automobile from the top of a neighbouring hill, hoping for a clear shot with no bystanders nearby. The first armour-piercing missile was aimed for Halawa's windshield, but he must have seen it coming since he opened his door and tried to get out. He wasn't quick enough. The missile exploded, throwing him from the automobile. The force of the boom shook my automobile, which was parked several hundred yards away. A second rocket was shot down and landed on the roadway. Halawa was in flames, as was the Golf, but he wasn't dead. My heart practically thumped out of my chest as I saw him flee through the streets, screaming in agony as the flames enveloped his body.

What exactly had we done?

When the Shin Bet saw my automobile so near to the scene, they yelled at me through my cell phone, "What are you doing!" "Would you like to be killed?" "Get the hell out of there!"

Despite the fact that I was not supposed to be anywhere near the attack location, I drove down to observe what would happen. I felt obligated and responsible to examine what I was a part of. It was truly ridiculous. If I had been discovered, it would have been too coincidental for anybody to believe that I wasn't involved in the assassination attempt, and I would almost certainly have been exposed.

That evening, I went to the hospital with my father and Marwan Barghouti to see Halawa. I couldn't even look at him because his face was so badly burned. But it seems that he was too religious to die.

He went into hiding for several months, and I heard that he unintentionally shot himself and nearly died. Even yet, it was insufficient to slow him down. He simply continued to murder people. Then Loai called me one day.

"Where are you?" "I'm at home." "Okay, stay there."

I didn't inquire as to what was going on. I'd become accustomed to following Loai's orders. Loai called again a few hours later. Halawa had apparently eaten with several buddies at a fried chicken restaurant near my residence. An Israeli spy recognized him and confirmed his identity. When Halawa and his pals exited the restaurant, two helicopters appeared in the skies, launched their missiles, and that was the end of it.

Following Halawa's assassination, some Al-Aqsa Martyrs Brigades members went to that restaurant and discovered a seventeen-year-old boy who had been one of the last individuals to see Halawa before he got into his car. He was an orphan with no one to look after him. As a result, he was tortured and admitted to working with the Israelis. They shot him, strapped his body to the back of a car, hauled it through Ramallah's streets, and hung him from the square's tower.

At the same time, the media began screaming that Israel had attempted to kill Marwan Barghouti, which it had not. I was aware that the organisation had taken precautions to avoid murdering him. But because everyone believed the newspapers and Al-Jazeera, Marwan Barghouti sought to capitalise on the rumour. "Yes, they tried to assassinate me," he continued, "but I was too smart for them."

When Abdullah Barghouti received the story in prison, he believed it as well, and he sent a handful of his special bombs to Marwan's assistant to be used to exact dreadful vengeance on the Israelis. Marwan was touched by the gesture and felt grateful to Abdullah.

* * *

The entrance of Abdullah had signified a significant shift in the war between Israel and Palestine. First, his bombs were far more sophisticated and lethal than anything we had seen previously, putting Israel at jeopardy and increasing pressure on the administration to stop the bombers.

Second, the Al-Aqsa Intifada had spread outside Palestine. Barghouti was a foreigner who was born in Kuwait. Who knows what other threats Israel might face beyond its borders?

Third, Barghouti was not an easy person to hunt down. He was not a member of Hamas. He wasn't a personal assistant. He was simply Barghouti, an unidentified independent death machine.

Soon after Abdullah was apprehended, the PA asked Marwan to speak with him about any future assaults he might be planning.

"Okay," Marwan replied. "I'll have Hassan Yousef talk to him."

Marwan was aware of my father's strong feelings against political corruption and had heard of his efforts to broker a peace deal between Hamas and the PA. He contacted my father, who agreed to meet with Abdullah.

My father had never heard of Abdullah Barghouti, who was not a Hamas member. "If you have anything planned, you need to tell the PA so we can stop it for now and take off some of the pressure we're getting from Israel, at least for the next few weeks," he cautioned Abdullah. If another explosion occurs, such as at the Dolphinarium or Sbarro, Israel will enter the West Bank in force. They'll take you if they get rough with the PA leaders."

Abdullah admitted sending multiple bombs to Nablus, where fighters planned to place the explosives into four cars, surround and assassinate Israeli Foreign Minister Shimon Peres while he was travelling. He also disclosed that Hamas operatives in the north planned to blow up a number of Israeli legislators. Unfortunately, he had no idea who the bombers were, who they had targeted, or who was plotting to kill Peres. He simply had a phone number.

My father returned home and told me what he had learned. We now had knowledge of a conspiracy to assassinate one of Israel's highest-ranking officials, the foreign minister. The implications were terrifying.

There was obviously nothing else to do but phone Abdullah's contact. Abdullah was not allowed to use Marwan Barghouti's phone, and my father was not allowed to use his either. We were all aware that the Israelis were listening in, and neither man wanted to be associated with the terrorist operations.

So my father sent me out to get a throwaway cell phone so we could make the call before throwing it away. I purchased the phone, took down the number, and reported it to the Shin Bet so that they could track the call.

Abdullah called his contact in Nablus and urged him to cease doing whatever he was doing until he received further instructions. When Israeli intelligence realised what was intended, they increased protection for every member of the Knesset and government. After a few months, things began to settle down a little.

Meanwhile, Marwan worked to secure Abdullah's release, not only because Abdullah had supplied him with bombs, but also because he wanted him free to kill more Israelis. Marwan Barghouti was a terrorist who personally shot soldiers and settlers in addition to being one of the commanders of the Second Intifada.

Abdullah Barghouti was eventually released by the PA. The Shin Bet was enraged.

Then everything went insane.

Chapter 19: The Game

On August 27, 2001, an Israeli helicopter launched two rockets at the office of PFLP Secretary-General Abu Ali Mustafa. As he sat at his desk, one of the rockets struck him.

More than 50,000 enraged Palestinians, including Mustafa's family, attended his funeral the next day. Mustafa had been a vocal opponent of the peace process and the Oslo Accords. Nonetheless, he was a moderate, like my father, and we had gone to hear him lecture many times together.

Israel falsely accused him of carrying out nine car bomb strikes. He was a political leader, not a military leader, like my father. Israel had zero proof against him. That I was certain of. It didn't matter, though. They assassinated Mustafa nevertheless, either in vengeance for the slaughter at the Sbarro restaurant, or possibly as a result of the Dolphinarium atrocity. They most likely only intended to send a message to Yasser Arafat. Mustafa was a member of the PLO's Executive Committee in addition to his membership in the PFLP.

On September 11, two weeks later, nineteen Al-Qaeda terrorists hijacked four commercial jetliners in the United States. Two planes collided with the World Trade Center in New York City. Another plane collided with the Pentagon in Washington. The fourth was discovered in a field in Somerset County, Pennsylvania. In addition to the terrorists, 2,973 others were killed.

As the news media tried to keep up with the astonishing events that were unfolding, I sat with the rest of the world, watching stories of the Twin Towers collapsing and white ash filling Church Street like a February blizzard. When I saw the footage of Palestinian youngsters rejoicing in the streets of Gaza, I felt a surge of shame.

The attack also reduced the Palestinian cause to ashes, as the world united in its condemnation of terrorism—any terrorism, for any cause. In the weeks that followed, the Shin Bet began looking for lessons in the rubble of what would become known simply as 9/11.

Why hadn't the US intelligence services been able to stop the disaster? For one thing, they were autonomous and competitive. For another thing, they relied heavily on technology and rarely worked with terrorists. Those techniques may have worked well during the Cold War, but it's difficult to confront obsessive principles with technology.

Israeli intelligence, on the other hand, depended mostly on human resources; it had a plethora of spies embedded in mosques, Islamic groups, and positions of authority; and it had little trouble recruiting even the most deadly terrorists. They realised they needed inside eyes and ears, as well as minds that understood motives and emotions and could connect the dots.

America had little understanding of Islamic culture or theology. Because of this, as well as free borders and inadequate security, it was an easier target than Israel. Even so, while my job as a spy enabled Israel to apprehend hundreds of terrorists, our efforts could not begin to put an end to terrorism—even in a small country like Israel.

On October 17, about a month later, four PFLP gunmen stormed the Jerusalem Hyatt Hotel and assassinated Israeli Tourism Minister Rehavam Ze'evi. They claimed it was in retaliation for the assassination of Mustafa. Ze'evi was an obvious target, despite his supposedly apolitical portfolio. He publicly proposed a program of making living in the West Bank and Gaza so difficult that the three million Palestinians there would willingly relocate to neighbouring Arab countries. Using metaphors, Ze'evi allegedly told an Associated Press reporter that some Palestinians were like "lice" that needed to be stopped like a "cancer spreading within us."

Tit for tat, the retaliatory slaughter went on. An eye for an eye—and there were plenty of them.

For several years, I had worked tirelessly to obtain any and all information I could to assist the Shin Bet in stopping the slaughter. We kept a watch on Muhammad Jamal al-Natsheh, Saleh Talahme, and the other three guys I had hidden away after they were released from the PA jail facility. They moved multiple times, and only Saleh stayed in touch with me. We tracked the others through their families and by listening in on public phone calls.

Saleh had faith in me, always told me where he lived, and constantly offered me to come. I grew to enjoy Saleh as I got to know him better. He was an incredible man—a great scholar who graduated at the top of his electrical engineering class and was one of Birzeit University's best students in its history. To him, I was Hassan Yousef's son, a good friend and listener.

When I told Loai and the other Shin Bet members about it, they were overjoyed. They reasoned that these coaching sessions would provide an excellent cover for intelligence gathering.

But it wasn't completely a cover. Saleh and I were becoming close. He taught me, and I did extremely well on the exam a few weeks later. I adored him, as well as his children. I frequently ate with the family, and a deep bond formed between all of us over time. It was an odd friendship since I knew Saleh had become a very dangerous man by this point. But then, I had done the same thing.

* * *

I was sitting at home one night in March 2002 when two men knocked on the door.

What am I going to do with a car filled with bombs, I wondered? I had to act swiftly. I made the decision to keep their automobile in the garage next to our house. It was clearly not one of my finer ideas, but I was compelled to think quickly.

I contacted Loai after they left, and to my relief, the Shin Bet arrived and towed the car away.

All five suicide bombers returned shortly afterwards. "All right," I said, "from now on, I'm your link to Hamas." I will give you all of your targets, places, and transportation. Do not communicate with anyone else, otherwise you may perish before you have a chance to kill any Israelis."

This circumstance provided an exceptional intelligence windfall. Nobody knew about suicide bombers before they detonated their bombs until now. Five of them showed up at my door with a carload of bombs. Prime Minister Sharon sanctioned their assassinations thirty minutes after I informed the Shin Bet of their location.

"Arrest them," I said, even though I knew it was a foolish idea even as I said it. Even when we had the car and the bombs, these guys were still wearing their belts. If a soldier got within a hundred yards of their one-room flat, the belts would detonate, taking everyone with them.

Even if we managed to get them out alive without killing anyone else, they'd be sure to give my name to their interrogators, and I'd be torched. Self-preservation informed me that the best thing for everyone involved would be for a chopper to drop a couple of missiles into their residence and call it a day.

My conscience, on the other hand, was being rewired. Though I was not yet a Christian, I was sincerely attempting to follow Jesus' ethical ideals. Allah had no objections to murder; in fact, he encouraged it. But Jesus had a much greater standard for me. I discovered that I couldn't even kill a terrorist.

At the same time, the Shin Bet had become far too valuable for them to risk losing me. They weren't pleased, but they eventually agreed to call off the assassination.

Troops from the security forces arrived on March 16. Because the bombers were in the heart of Ramallah, the IDF was unable to bring in tanks. The operation was extremely risky because the men had to enter on foot. I watched the events unfold from my home while Loai called me and kept me up to date on everything that was going on.

We all waited till we heard snoring on the monitors.

The biggest danger was rousing them up too soon. Before any bomber could move a muscle, the troops had to get through the entrance and to the beds.

As we listened to the monitors for the smallest disturbance, the least pause in the sleep, a soldier attached an explosive charge to the door. They then gave the command.

The door blew up. Special forces commandos stormed the small apartment, apprehending all but one of the men. He grabbed a gun and leaped through the window, killing himself before he struck the ground.

Everyone let out a relieved sigh. Everyone but me. As soon as the boys were loaded into the vehicle, one of them mentioned my name, revealing me as a collaborator.

My worst nightmare had come true. I was scorched. What happens next?

Loai had the answer. The Shin Bet simply deported the man back to Jordan, imprisoning his pals. So, when he was at home, enjoying himself with his family, the other three would conclude he was the traitor, not me. It was fantastic.

I'd gotten away with it one more time, but only just. But it was obvious that I was pushing my luck a little too far.

* * *

One day, I received a letter from Shin Bet chairman Avi Dichter praising me for my efforts on their behalf. He claimed to have accessed all of Israel's anti-terrorism files and discovered the Green Prince in each one. This was both flattering and forewarning. It was acknowledged by both myself and Loai. If I kept moving in the same direction, I'd die. The path out there was far too long. Someone was certain to come across it. I needed to be cleaned in some way.

My obstinate refusal to allow the five suicide bombers to be murdered had severely jeopardized my situation. Even though everyone assumed that the bomber who had been returned to Jordan was responsible for the arrests, they also understood that Israel will not hesitate to arrest anyone suspected of assisting suicide bombers. And I had been of great assistance to them. So how come I hadn't been arrested?

A week after the bombers were apprehended, the Israeli security team came up with two options that could spare my life. First, they may arrest me and re-arrest me. But I was scared that would be the same as giving my father the death penalty, as he would no longer have me to protect him from Israeli assassination attempts. "The other option is for us to play the game." "Game? "Which game?"

Loai indicated that we needed to stage a high-profile incident that would persuade all of Palestine that Israel wanted me jailed or killed. It couldn't be staged in order to appear convincing. It had to be true. The Israeli Defense Forces had to make a concerted effort to apprehend me. As a result, the Shin Bet was forced to influence and deceive the IDF—their own people.

The IDF had only a few hours to prepare for this huge operation, according to the Shin Bet. They cautioned me that as Hassan Yousef's son, I was a very dangerous young man since I had a close association with suicide bombers and might be armed with explosives. They said they had good information that I would see my mother that night at my father's residence. I would only be there for a short time and would be equipped with an M16.

What a buildup they provided. It was a complicated game.

The IDF was led to believe that I was a high-profile terrorist who could vanish forever if they made a mistake. So they did everything they could to prevent that from happening. Undercover special troops disguised as Arabs, accompanied by highly trained snipers, reached the area in Palestinian vehicles, came to a halt two minutes from the residence, and waited for a signal. Heavy tanks were stationed near the territorial border fifteen minutes distant. In case of difficulties with Palestinian street combatants, helicopter gunships were ready to give air cover.

I sat in my car outside my father's house, waiting for a call from the Shin Bet. When it arrived, I'd have sixty seconds to flee before the special forces surrounded the house. On my end, there was no room for error.

I felt a pang of sorrow as I pictured how afraid my mother and younger siblings would be in a matter of seconds. They would have to pay the price for whatever my father and I did, as was customary.

I looked out at my mother's lovely garden. She'd collected flowers from all over the place, taking cuttings from friends and family wherever she could. She treated her flowers as if they were her children.

"How many flowers do we need?" I used to make fun of her. "Just a few more," was the standard response.

I remembered her pointing to one and saying, "This plant is older than you." You smashed its pot as a child, but I preserved it and it's still alive."

Will it be alive in a few minutes after arriving troops crush it under their feet?

My phone began to ring.

My head was filled with blood. My heart was pounding. I started my car and drove into the middle of town, where I had set up a new secret site. I was no longer posing as a fugitive. Soldiers who would rather kill me than arrest me were on the lookout for me at the time. Ten civilian cars with Palestinian licence plates slammed on their brakes one minute after my departure. The residence was encircled by Israeli special forces, with automatic weapons covering every entrance and window. My brother Naser was among the many children in the neighbourhood. They stopped playing soccer and ran away, afraid.

More than twenty tanks rolled in as soon as the infantry were in place. The entire city was now aware that something was wrong. I could hear the enormous diesel engines from where I was hiding. Hundreds of armed Palestinian militants stormed my father's house, encircling the IDF. They couldn't shoot, however, because children were still scrambling for cover and my family was inside.

The helicopters were summoned when the fedayeen arrived.

I now wondered if I had made a mistake by sparing the suicide bombers. My family and our neighbourhood would not be in danger if I had simply let the IDF drop a bomb on them. I would never forgive myself if one of my siblings died in this mayhem.

To ensure that our complex production became a global news story, I had informed Al-Jazeera that an attack on Sheikh Hassan Yousef's home was planned. They were all certain that the Israelis had finally apprehended my father and planned to broadcast his arrest live. I imagined their reaction when the loudspeakers began to crackle and the troops ordered his oldest son, Mosab, to come out with his hands up. As soon as I arrived at my place, I turned on the television and joined the rest of the Arab world in watching the drama.

My family was evacuated and questioned by the soldiers. My mother informed them that I had left one minute prior to their arrival. They, of course, did not believe her. They trusted the Shin Bet, who had produced the entire production and were the only people other than myself who knew the game had begun. They threatened to start firing if I didn't surrender.Everyone waited for me to come out for 10 minutes, and if I did, whether I would come out shooting or with my hands in the air. Then time ran out. They opened fire, and over 200 bullets pierced my second-floor bedroom (and are still embedded in the walls today). There was no more conversation. They'd definitely be determined to murder me.

The gunshots abruptly came to a halt. A missile whistled through the air and blew out half our house moments later. Soldiers stormed inside. I knew they were going through every room. There was no body and no fugitive in hiding.

The IDF felt humiliated and outraged that I had escaped their grasp. Loai said over the phone that if they caught me now, they would shoot me on sight. However, the operation was a success for us. Nobody had been wounded, and I had risen to the top of the wanted list. The entire city was abuzz about me. I'd transformed into a dangerous terrorist overnight.

For the next few months, I had three goals: stay out of the army's way, protect my father, and keep gathering intelligence. That is the order.

Chapter 20: Defensive Shield

The violence spiralled out of control.

Israelis were shot, stabbed, and bombed. Palestinians were murdered. It spun round and round, faster and faster. The international community attempted in vain to exert pressure on Israel.

"End the illegal occupation... Stop bombing civilian areas, assassinations, the unnecessary use of lethal force, demolitions, and the daily humiliation of ordinary Palestinians," UN Secretary-General Kofi Annan stated in March 2002.

On the same day that we apprehended the four suicide bombers I had protected from killing, European Union leaders urged both Israel and the Palestinians to calm down. "There is no military solution to this conflict," that's what they said.

Passover fell on March 27, 2002. 250 guests had assembled for the customary Seder lunch in a dining room on the ground level of the Park Hotel in Netanya.

On March 29, I checked into the City Inn Hotel on Nablus Road in Al-Bireh, which housed the BBC, CNN, and other international media. My father and I communicated using two-way radios.

The Shin Bet anticipated that I would be at my hotel, eating chips and watching TV. But I didn't want to miss out on anything so crucial. I needed to be on top of things, so I slung my M16 over my shoulder and went outside. I climbed to the top of the hill close to the Ramallah Library, from where I could view the southeast part of town, where my father was. I felt I'd be safe there, and I'd be able to flee to the hotel as soon as I heard the tanks.

Hundreds of Merkavas stormed into the city around midnight. I hadn't anticipated them to attack from all sides at once, let alone move that swiftly. Some of the streets were so small that tank drivers had to climb over the tops of the automobiles. Other streets were sufficiently wide, but the soldiers appeared to love the shriek of grinding metal beneath their feet. Streets in the refugee camps were barely more than walkways between cinder-block houses that had been beaten into gravel by the tanks.

I'd parked my father's Audi on the street. And I stood there in awe as a tank tread crushed it to pulp. It wasn't meant to be there. I had no idea what to do. I couldn't phone Loai and ask him to halt the operation since I'd decided to play Rambo.

I dashed toward the city centre and dived into an underground parking garage, barely yards from an approaching tank. There were no troops on the ground yet since they were waiting for the Merkavas to secure the region. I had a scary realisation all of a sudden. In the building just over my head, several Palestinian resistance outfits had offices. I'd sought sanctuary in a vital objective.

Tanks lack discernment. They are unable to distinguish between Shin Bet collaborators and terrorists, Christians and Muslims, armed warriors and defenceless citizens. And the children within those machines were as terrified as I was. Guys who looked exactly like me shot AK-47s at the tanks all around me. Ping, ping, and ping. The bullets bounced around like toys. BOOM! The tank yelled back, almost breaking my eardrums.

Massive chunks of the buildings surrounding us began to crumble into smouldering piles. Every cannon bang was a stomach punch. Every wall rang with the clamour of automatic rifles. Another detonation. Dust clouds that are blinding. Stone and metal fragments flew everywhere.

I needed to get out of there as soon as possible. But how exactly?

Suddenly, a swarm of Fatah fighters charged into the garage and huddled around me. This was not a good sign. What if the army arrived right now? The fedayeen would attack them. Would I also shoot? If so, who is it aimed at? They'd kill me even if I didn't shoot. But I couldn't murder anyone. I might have been able to do so once, but not any longer.

More fighters arrived, screaming out to others as they fled. Everything appeared to come to a halt. Nobody took a breath.

IDF soldiers entered the garage with caution. Closer. Whatever was about to happen will happen in a matter of seconds. Their torches looked for the whites of eyes or a weapon's reflection. They paid attention. And we stood there watching. Both sides' sweaty index fingers were poised on triggers.

The Red Sea then divided.

Perhaps they were terrified to venture any further into the dark, humid parking garage, or perhaps they simply desired the comfortable company of a tank. For some reason, the soldiers came to a halt, turned, and simply walked away. When they were done, I went upstairs and located a room where I could call Loai.

There was an awkward silence. "Okay, we'll see what we can do."

It took several hours to move the tanks and men, who must have been perplexed as to why they had been called back. I nearly broke my leg jumping from one rooftop to another to get back to my room after they moved. I slammed the door shut, stripped naked, and shoved my terrorist outfit and weapon into the air-conditioning vent.

Meanwhile, my father's hiding place was right in the middle of the storm. The IDF examined every house in his vicinity, behind every building, and behind every rock. However, they were not permitted to enter that particular house.

Inside, my father prayed and read the Qur'an. The house's owner prayed and read the Qur'an. His wife prayed and read the Qur'an. The troops then left for no apparent reason and began scouring another location.

"You will not believe the miracle, Mosab!" my father remarked later into my phone. "It was incredible! They arrived. They searched every house in the neighbourhood except where we were. "All praise to Allah!"

You're welcome, I reasoned.

Nothing like Operation Defensive Shield had occurred since the Six-Day War. And this was just the start. Ramallah was at the helm of the operation. Bethlehem, Jenin, and Nablus were next. The IDF had encircled Yasser Arafat's compound while I was rushing around escaping Israeli forces. Everything was secured. Curfews were strictly enforced.

Tanks and armoured personnel carriers surrounded the Preventive Security Compound near our home in Betunia on April 2. Helicopter gunships circled above. The Shin Bet was frustrated because it was coming up empty-handed everywhere else, and we knew the PA was sheltering at least fifty wanted men at the site.

In addition to the four-story office structure that housed Colonel Jibril Rajoub11 and other security personnel, the site featured four buildings. The CIA had designed, built, and outfitted the entire facility. The CIA trained and armed the cops. There were even CIA offices there. Inside were hundreds of heavily armed police officers, as well as a considerable number of convicts, including Bilal Barghouti and others on Israel's target list. The Shin Bet and IDF were taking no prisoners. The army stated over the loudspeakers that it would blow up Building One in five minutes and ordered everyone out.

Building Two went up exactly five minutes later. "Everybody out!"

Building Three is complete. Building Four has gone up in flames. Boom!

"Take off your clothes!" exclaimed the loudspeakers. The Israelis did not take any chances that someone was still armed or packed with bombs. Hundreds of men stripped naked on the street. They were given jumpsuits, put onto buses, and transported to the neighbouring Ofer Military Base, where the Shin Bet realised its error.

Of course, there were too many people to lock up, but the Israelis were only interested in the fugitives. They intended to sort through the inmates and release everyone save those on the list of suspects. The issue was that everyone had left their clothes—along with their ID cards—at the compound. How would the security personnel tell the difference between wanted men and police?

Louis' boss, Ofer Dekel, was in control. He dialled Jibril Rajoub's number, who was away from the property at the time of the incident. Dekel granted Rajoub a special permit, allowing him to safely travel between hundreds of tanks and thousands of soldiers. When Dekel came, he asked Rajoub whether he could tell him which persons worked for him and which were fugitives. Rajoub stated that he would be delighted to. Rajoub quickly identified police as fugitives and fugitives as police, and the Shin Bet quickly freed all of the sought men.

"Why did you do that to me?" Dekel inquired after determining what had occurred.

"You just blew up my offices and compound," Rajoub remarked casually, sounding like a Palestinian version of "Duh." Dekel also appeared to have forgotten that his PA pal had been injured a year before when IDF tanks and helicopters wrecked his home, leaving him even less willing to offer favours for the Israelis.

The Shin Bet was profoundly humiliated. In retaliation, the only thing they could do was release an official report labelling Rajoub a traitor for turning over the wanted individuals to Israel in a deal organised by the CIA. As a result, Rajoub lost control and became the president of the Palestinian Soccer Association.

This was obviously a disaster.

The Israelis did occasionally suspend the curfew during the next three weeks, and during a respite on April 15, I was able to carry some food and other supplies to my father. He said he didn't feel comfortable in that residence and that he wanted to leave. I called one of Hamas' commanders and inquired if he knew of any safe haven for Hassan Yousef. He urged me to take my father to the hideout of Sheikh Jamal al-Taweel, another high-profile Hamas fugitive.

I was astounded. The arrest of Jamal al-Taweel would undoubtedly boost the Shin Bet's confidence in Operation Defensive Shield. "Let's not put my father in the same place," I added as I thanked him. It could be too risky for both of them to be there at the same time." We decided on another location, and I swiftly moved my father into his new safe haven. Then I dialled Loai's number.

"I know where Jamal al-Taweel is hiding."

Loai couldn't believe it when he learned that al-Taweel had been arrested that very night. On the same day, we apprehended Marwan Barghouti, another of the IDF's most sought men.

Marwan was one of Hamas' most elusive leaders, yet his capture was actually relatively simple. I contacted one of his bodyguards and spoke briefly with him on his cell phone while the Shin Bet traced the conversation. After being convicted in a civilian court, Barghouti was condemned to five consecutive life terms.

Meanwhile, not a single day went by without Operation Defensive

Shield making international headlines. Few were complimentary. Rumours of a large-scale massacre emerged from Jenin, which no one could confirm because the IDF had sealed the city. According to Palestinian cabinet minister Saeb Erekat, 500 people were killed. The number was later reduced to around 50.

For almost five weeks, more than 200 Palestinians were held hostage in Bethlehem's Church of the Nativity. After the dust settled and most residents were permitted to go, 8 Palestinians were killed, 26 were taken to Gaza, 85 were checked and freed by the IDF, and the 13 most wanted were banished to Europe.

In total, almost 500 Palestinians were murdered, 1,500 were injured, and nearly 4,300 were imprisoned by the IDF during Defensive Shield. On the other hand, 29 Israelis were killed and 127 were injured. The World Bank projected the damage to be in excess of $360 million.

Chapter 21: Supernatural Protection

The 31st of July, 2002, was a scorcher. The temperature is 122 degrees Fahrenheit. There were no lessons on Hebrew University's Mount Scopus campus, while some students were still taking exams. Others waited in line to sign up for September classes. At 1:30 p.m., the Frank Sinatra Cafeteria at the campus was full with people cooling off, drinking iced tea, and chatting. Nobody saw the package that a contract painter had left there.

The enormous explosion destroyed the cafeteria and killed nine individuals, five of them were Americans. Eighty-five additional people were injured, fourteen of them badly.

* * *

I also required emotional assistance. The loneliness was excruciating. In my own city, I had become a foreigner. I couldn't tell anyone about my life, not even my own family. And I couldn't put my trust in anyone else. Loai and I usually met at one of the Shin Bet safe houses in Jerusalem. But I couldn't get out of Ramallah any longer. Even walking down the street during the day was dangerous. None of the normal choices were available.

If special forces arrived in Palestinian cars to pick me up, they risked being stopped by fedayeen and their accents exposing them. Someone could see me jumping into the jeep if security agents in IDF clothes claimed to kidnap me. And even if it worked, how many times could we pull it off?

Finally, the Shin Bet devised a more inventive manner for us to meet. Ofer Military Base, located a few miles south of Ramallah, was one of Israel's most secure locations. The facility was densely packed with secrets and heavily guarded. Local Shin Bet offices were present.

The strategy was concerning. And when it came time to put it into action late one night, I felt like an actor on opening night, about to walk onto a set he'd never seen before, dressed in a costume he'd never worn before, with no script and no rehearsal.

I had no idea the Shin Bet had their own agents stationed in the two guard towers bordering the point on the outer perimeter that I was intended to penetrate. I also had no idea that extra armed security personnel outfitted with night-vision equipment were stationed along my route to defend me in the improbable case that I was being followed.

What if I make a mistake? I kept thinking.

My car was parked out of sight. Loai had told me to dress in black clothes, not bring a flashlight, and to bring a pair of bolt cutters. I inhaled deeply.

I could see the twinkling of the base lights in the distance as I drove into the hills. As I followed the rise and fall of the steep terrain, a gang of stray dogs growled at my heels for a time. That was fine as long as they didn't attract unwanted attention.

Finally, I reached the outer fence and summoned Loai.

"From the corner, count seven stanchions," he went on to say. "Then wait for my sign and start cutting."

I cut through what had become the old fence after a new one approximately twenty feet inside had been installed at the start of the Second Intifada.

I'd been warned about guard pigs (yeah, I said guard pigs), but I didn't come across any, so it didn't matter. The area between the outer and inner perimeters formed a run that would be patrolled by German shepherds or other highly trained attack dogs at any other military base in the globe. The kosher-conscious Israelis, ironically, employed pigs. That is correct.

The presence of pigs and the danger of interaction with them was supposed to serve as a psychological barrier to any prospective terrorist who was a devout Muslim. Both Islam and Orthodox Judaism strictly prohibit interaction with pigs. Maybe even more so.

I never saw pigs defending a settlement, but Loai later told me that they served as sentries at Ofer Military Base.

I discovered an unsecured little entrance in the inner fence. I passed through, and there I was, inside one of Israel's most secure military stations, with guard towers rearing up on either side like the devil's horns.

I always brought them recording devices, evidence, or intelligence, but this time I was empty-handed.

We dashed up and over a hill to an area where two jeeps were waiting. Three of the men got into the first vehicle, and I got in the rear. The others remained in the second jeep to ensure my safe return. I felt bad for the folks we left behind because it was pouring buckets. But they appeared to be having a good time.

I left after meeting with Loai, his employer, and the guards for a few hours, pleased with myself despite the lengthy, rainy, and chilly journey back.

This became our normal meeting format. It was wonderfully choreographed and executed every time. I never had to cut the fence again, but I kept the cutters on hand just in case.

* * *

After my "escape" from the extremely apparent IDF raid, I continued to check in on my father to see if he was okay and if he needed anything. I stopped by the USAID office every now and again, but since we had halted most of our work, I was able to complete what little I needed to do from my computer at home. I hung out with wanted people at night to acquire intelligence. And sometimes or twice a month, I penetrate a top-secret military installation late at night to attend a meeting.

In my leisure time, I continued to meet with my Christian friends to talk about Jesus' love. Actually, it was much more than just chatter. Even though I was only a student of the Teacher, I felt God's love and protection every day, and it appeared to extend to the members of my family as well.

When special forces troops searched the City Inn for fugitives and came up empty, they chose to rest at a nearby property. This was standard procedure. Orders or authorization were not required by the IDF. When things were quiet, their special forces soldiers just took over someone's residence to get a few hours of relaxation and possibly something to eat. During severe battle, they would break into nearby homes and utilise the residents as human shields, just like the fedayeen did.

They chose the house where my father was hiding on this particular day. The Shin Bet had no idea what was going on. Neither did any of us. Nobody could have predicted or stopped the soldiers' choice of that particular residence on that particular day. My father "happened" to be in the basement when they arrived.

"Could you please not bring the dogs in here?" said the woman who lived there. "I have little children."

Her husband was frightened that the army would find Hassan Yousef and arrest them for sheltering a wanted person. So he pretended to be normal and unafraid. He directed his seven-year-old daughter to approach the commander and shake his hand. The commander was taken by the small girl and assumed she and her parents were ordinary people with nothing to do with terrorists. He respectfully asked the woman if his guys might rest upstairs for a few minutes, and she responded it was alright. Twenty-five Israeli troops sat in the house for over eight hours, completely oblivious that my father was physically beneath them.

I couldn't shake the feeling of supernatural protection and intervention. It felt genuine to me. When Ahmad al-Faransi called from the centre of Ramallah, asking if I could pick him up and drive him home, I assured him I was in the neighbourhood and would be there in a few minutes. When I arrived, he got into the car and we began driving.

We hadn't gone very far when al-Faransi's phone rang. Al-Faransi was on the hit list in Jerusalem, and Arafat's headquarters was ringing to tell him that Israeli helicopters were following him. When I opened the window, I heard two Apaches approaching. Though it may appear weird to those who have never heard God speak to them in an internal voice, I heard God speak to my heart on this day, ordering me to turn left between two buildings. I later discovered that if I had continued straight, the Israelis would have had a clear shot at my car. When I turned the automobile, I heard that supernatural voice say, "Get out of the car and leave it." We leaped out and took off running. When the chopper re-acquired its objective, all it could see was a parked car and two open doors. It hovered for almost sixty seconds before turning and flying away.

Later, I discovered that intelligence had gotten word that al-Faransi had been seen getting into a dark blue Audi A4. There were a lot of them throughout town. Loai wasn't in the operations room at the time to check my whereabouts, and no one thought to question if this Audi belonged to the Green Prince. Few Shin Bet agents were even aware of my presence.

I always seemed to be blessed with heavenly protection. I wasn't even a Christian yet, and al-Faransi had never heard of the Lord. My Christian friends, on the other hand, prayed for me every day. And God, according to Jesus in Matthew 5:45, "causes his sun to rise on the evil and the good, and sends rain on the righteous and the unrighteous." This was a far cry from the Qur'anic god of cruelty and vengeance.

Chapter 22: Protective Custody

I was completely fatigued. I was sick of playing so many dangerous parts at once, and I was sick of having to modify my attitude and appearance to fit the current organisation I was working for. When I was with my father and other Hamas leaders, I had to act like a devoted Hamas member. I had to assume the role of an Israeli collaborator while working with the Shin Bet. At home, I frequently played the role of father and guardian of my siblings, and at work, I had to play the role of an ordinary working person. I was in my final semester of college and had examinations to prepare for. But I was unable to concentrate.

It was the end of September 2002, and I thought it was time for act 2 of the play, which had begun with the Shin Bet's bogus arrest attempt.

I told my mother where my father was hiding and allowed her to pay him a visit. Special soldiers descended on the area five minutes after she arrived at the safe home. Soldiers went through the neighbourhood, yelling at citizens to come inside.

One of those "civilians," smoking a narghile (Turkish water pipe) in front of his house, was master bomb maker Abdullah Barghouti, who had no idea he was living across the street from Hassan Yousef. And the hapless IDF soldier who ordered him inside had no idea he was yelling at Israel's most wanted mass murderer.

Everyone was in the dark. My father had no idea his son had handed him up to shield him from assassination. And the IDF had no knowledge that the Shin Bet had known Hassan Yousef's whereabouts all along, and that some of its soldiers had eaten lunch and napped in the house where he was hiding.

My father, as usual, surrendered gently. And he and the other Hamas officials felt the Shin Bet had tracked my mother down to her hiding place. My mother was naturally heartbroken, but she was also pleased that her husband was safe and no longer on Israel's hit list.

"We'll see you tonight," Loai said once the dust had settled.

I sat inside my house, peering out the window, as the sun began to drop on the horizon, watching as roughly twenty special forces personnel swept in quickly and took their positions. I realised I needed to put my head down and brace myself for some tough treatment. Jeeps arrived a few minutes later. Then there was a tank. The IDF cordoned off the area. Someone climbed onto my balcony. Someone else knocked on my door.

I'm not sure why they bothered to inquire. They began breaking down doors and scouring the house, room by room. I found myself outside, face to face with my pal.

When I encountered the interrogators, even those who had tormented me during my earlier incarceration, I was startled to find that I had no ill will toward them. I could only describe it using a passage I had read: According to Hebrews 4:12, "the word of God is alive and active." Sharper than any two-edged blade, it divides soul and spirit, joints and marrow, and judges the thoughts and attitudes of the heart." I'd read and studied these words, as well as Jesus' admonition to forgive your enemies and love those who abuse you, several times. Even though I couldn't embrace Jesus Christ as God, his teachings seemed to be alive, active, and acting inside me. I'm not sure how else I could have seen people as humans, not as Jews or Arabs, prisoners or torturers. Even the old animosity that drove me to acquire guns and plot Israeli assassination was being replaced by a love I didn't comprehend.

I was locked up in a cell by myself for a few weeks. My Shin Bet buddies came to check on me and chat once or twice a day, when they weren't busy interrogating other detainees. I ate well and managed to remain the prison's best-kept secret. There were no stinky hoods, insane hunchbacks, or Leonard Cohen tunes this time (though he would eventually become my favourite recorded artist—weird, huh?). In the West Bank, word got around that I was a tough guy who refused to give Israelis any information, even when tortured.

I was put into my father's cell a few days before my transfer. My father's face lit up with relief as he extended his arms for an embrace. He smirked as he pushed me away from him.

"I followed you," I chuckled. "I couldn't live without you."

We laughed around and had a fantastic time in the cell with two other people. To be honest, I was relieved to see my father safely imprisoned.

There would be no errors. No rockets would be launched from the skies. I used to just stare at him and listen to his wonderful voice while he read the Qur'an to us. I remembered how gentle dad was when we were kids. He never made us get out of bed for early morning prayers, but we all did it to make him proud. He had devoted his life to Allah at a young age and had demonstrated his dedication to the rest of us.

Now I said to myself, "My beloved father, I am so happy to be sitting here with you." I realise prison is the last place you want to be right now, but your broken remains would most likely be in a little vinyl bag somewhere if you weren't here. When he looked up, he saw me gazing lovingly and appreciatively at him. He didn't understand why, and I couldn't explain it to him.

When the guards arrived to take me away, my father and I gripped warmly. He appeared fragile in my arms, but I knew how powerful he was. We'd been so close the previous three days that I felt like I was being torn apart. It was extremely tough for me to leave the Shin Bet officials. Over the years, we had grown exceedingly close. I gazed at their expressions, hoping they realised how much I admired them. They returned my sorry glance. They knew the following stop on my route would be difficult.

The soldiers who shackled me for transfer had radically opposite expressions. To them, I was a terrorist who had escaped the IDF, embarrassed them, and avoided capture. This time, I was transferred to Ofer Prison, which was part of the military base where I had been meeting with the Shin Bet on a regular basis.

My beard, like everyone else's, grew long and thick. And I went about my usual business with the other convicts. When it was time for prayer, I bowed, knelt, and prayed, but not to Allah. I prayed to the Creator of the Universe right now. I was getting there. I even discovered an Arabic-language Bible in the library's world religion section one day. It was the entire package, not just the New Testament. It had never been touched. I'm sure no one knew it was there. What a lovely gift! I read it several times. Every now and then, someone would approach me and gently inquire as to what I was doing. I mentioned that I studied history and that, being an ancient text, the Bible included some of the earliest knowledge known. Not only that, but the morals it imparts are excellent, and I feel that every Muslim should read it. Most people were fine with it. The only time they hurt was during Ramadan, when I seemed to be reading the Bible more than the Qur'an.

A second notice arrived. Then another.

Amnon was arrested and imprisoned after continuing to refuse to serve. What I didn't realise was that Amnon had spent the entire time I was at Ofer in the Jewish portion of the prison. He was there because he refused to collaborate with the Israelis, and I was there because I consented to. I was attempting to safeguard Jews, while he was attempting to protect Palestinians.

I didn't feel that everyone in Israel and the occupied territories had to become Christians in order to put an end to the violence. But I figured a thousand Amnons on one side and a thousand Mosabs on the other could make a major impact. And what if we had more... Who knows?

I was taken to court a few months after arriving at Ofer, where no one knew who I was—not the judge, nor the prosecution, not even my own counsel.

The Shin Bet testified at my trial that I was dangerous and that I should be detained longer. The judge agreed and sentenced me to administrative detention for six months. I was transferred once more.

The tent jail of Ktzi'ot stood five hours drive from anywhere, in the sand dunes of the Negev Desert and very close to the Dimona nuclear reactor, where you melted in the summer and froze in the winter.

"What's your organisation?" "Hamas."

Yes, I still saw myself as a member of my family, as a part of my history. But I was not like the other inmates.

Hamas remained the majority. However, Fatah had grown greatly since the start of the Second Intifada, and each faction had roughly the same number of tents. I was sick of acting, and my newly discovered ethical code prohibited me from lying. So I planned to keep to myself as much as possible while I was there.

To keep the mouse population under control, the Israelis practically papered the camp with adhesive boards. I was reading my Bible early one chilly morning while everyone else was still sleeping when I heard a rusty bedspring-like creaking sound. When I investigated under my cot, I discovered a mouse tied to a glue board. What amazed me was that another mouse was attempting to save him without becoming entangled himself. Was it a friend or a mate? I'm not sure. I stood there for approximately a half hour, watching as one animal put its life in danger to save another. It moved me so greatly that I decided to set them both free.

Reading materials in the prison were mostly limited to the Qur'an and Qur'anic studies. I only had two English-language novels, which a friend had smuggled to me via my lawyer. I was grateful to have something to read and practise my English, but it didn't take long for me to wear out the covers from reading so much. I was going around by myself one day when I noticed two convicts brewing tea. A large wooden box beside them contained literature sent by the Red Cross. And these thugs were destroying the books for fuel! I couldn't keep myself in check. I pushed the box away from them and began picking up the books. They assumed I wanted them to prepare my own tea.

They were undoubtedly wondering what was wrong with Hassan Yousef's youth. He'd been so quiet, generally reading and keeping to himself. He was suddenly gushing over a box of books. If it had been anyone else, they would have struggled to protect their valuable fuel. They did, however, allow me to keep the novels, and I returned to my bed with a whole box of new treasures. I stacked them on top of each other and wallowed in them. I didn't care what other people thought. While I tried to pass the time in this spot, my heart was singing and praising God for supplying me with something to read.

I read for sixteen hours a day until my eyes became tired from the bad lighting. I memorised four thousand English vocabulary words during my four months at Ktzi'ot.

During my time there, I witnessed two prison riots that were even worse than the one at Megiddo. But God carried me through it all. In fact, I felt God's presence more intensely in that prison than at any other moment before or since. I didn't know Jesus as the Creator yet, but I was learning to love God the Father.

* * *

It was published on April 2, 2003, as Coalition ground troops raced toward Baghdad. I emerged as a respected Hamas leader, a seasoned terrorist, and a cunning fugitive. I'd been tested and proven by fire. My chances of being burned were greatly decreased, yet my father was still alive and well.

I could now walk freely through the streets of Ramallah. I no longer had to disguise myself as a fugitive. I could reclaim my identity. I dialled my mother's number, then Loads.

"Welcome home, Green Prince," he welcomed him. "We really missed you. A lot has been going on, and we weren't sure what to do without you."

I met up with Loai and other excellent Israeli pals a few days after my return. They only had one piece of news to report, but it was a big one.

Abdullah Barghouti was apprehended and detained in March. Later that year, the Kuwaiti-born bomb maker would be prosecuted in an Israeli military court for killing 66 people and injuring hundreds more. I knew there were more, but those were the only ones we could verify. Barghouti would be sentenced to 67 life terms, one for each murder victim and an additional one for all others he had injured. He would express no remorse, blame Israel, and regret only that he did not have the opportunity to kill more Jews at his sentence.

"The spate of murderous terror that the accused let loose was one of the most severe in the blood-soaked history of this country," the judges were quoted as saying.12 In a frenzy, Barghouti threatened to kill the judges and teach every Hamas prisoner how to construct explosives. As a result, he would be sentenced to solitary confinement. However, Ibrahim Hamed, my friend Saleh Talahme, and the rest remained at large.

My project at USAID, as well as my employment, terminated in October. So I poured myself into my Shin Bet work, acquiring all the information I could.

One morning, a few months later, Loai called. "We found Saleh."

Chapter 23: A Vision for Hamas

My father had had an epiphany during his most recent confinement. He'd always been a really open-minded person. He would sit down and converse with Christians, atheists, and even Jews. He paid close attention to journalists, experts, and analysts, and he attended university courses. And he paid attention to me as his assistant, adviser, and guardian. As a result, his vision was considerably clearer and larger than that of other Hamas leaders.

He saw Israel as an immovable reality and saw many of Hamas's aspirations as irrational and unrealistic. He wanted to find a happy medium that all parties could accept without losing face. So, in his first public speech after his release, he proposed a two-state solution to the dispute. Nothing like that had ever been spoken in Hamas. The closest they ever came to a handshake was a truce. But my father was truly recognizing Israel's right to exist! His phone didn't stop ringing.

Diplomats from every country, including the US, contacted us to arrange secret meetings with my father. They were curious to see if he was genuine. I was his translator, and I never left his side. My Christian friends totally backed him, and he adored them for it.

He, predictably, had an issue. He spoke in the name of Hamas, but he did not speak from the heart of Hamas. However, it would have been the worst conceivable time for him to leave the group. The death of Yasser Arafat left a big void, and the streets of the seized territories were boiling. Radical young men were everywhere—armed, hateful, and without a leader.

It's not that Arafat was impossible to replace. Any crooked politician would suffice. The issue was that he had consolidated the PA and the PLO fully. He wasn't a team player in the least. He had all the power and all the connections. And his name appeared on every bank account.

Fatah was now plagued with Arafat imposters. But who would be acceptable to Palestinians and the world community — and powerful enough to rule all factions? Even Arafat had never been able to accomplish this.

My father was less than thrilled when Hamas chose to run in the Palestinian parliamentary elections a few months later. He had seen Hamas transform into an ungainly creature with one extremely long militant leg and one very short political leg when the military wing was introduced during the Al-Aqsa Intifada. Hamas simply did not understand the rules of the game.

Being a revolutionary requires utmost purity and firmness. However, governing requires compromise and flexibility. Negotiation would not be an option if Hamas sought to rule; it would be required. They would suddenly be in charge of the budget, water, food, power, and waste removal as elected officials. And it all had to go via Israel. Any autonomous Palestinian state would be required to be cooperative.

My father recalled his discussions with Western leaders and how Hamas rejected every suggestion. It was automatically pessimistic and contrarian. And, since it refused to engage with the Americans and Europeans, my father reasoned, what chance did an elected Hamas have of sitting down at the table with the Israelis?

My father didn't mind if Hamas ran candidates. He just did not want to fill the ticket with high-profile leaders like himself, whom the people loved and appreciated. He was afraid that if that happened, Hamas would win. And he was well aware that a Hamas win would be disastrous for the people. He was confirmed correct by events.

"There certainly exists among us concern that Israel, and perhaps others also, will impose punishments on the Palestinians because they voted for Hamas," he was quoted as saying by Haaretz. "They will say 'you decided to choose Hamas and therefore we will intensify the siege over you and make your lives difficult.'"

Many in Hamas, however, smelt money, power, and glory. Former leaders who had abandoned the organisation appeared out of nowhere to claim a piece of the pie. Their selfishness, recklessness, and ignorance horrified my father. They didn't know the difference between the CIA and USAID. Who was supposed to collaborate with them?

* * *

I was dissatisfied with almost everything. I was fed up with the PA's corruption, Hamas' ineptitude and cruelty, and the seemingly never-ending list of terrorists who needed to be apprehended or killed. The pretence and risk that had become my daily ritual were wearing on me. I desired a normal existence.

One day in August, while walking through the streets of Ramallah, I noticed a man bringing a computer up a flight of steps to a repair business. And it dawned to me that there could be a demand for in-home computer servicing, similar to the American Geek Squad. I figured that because I was no longer working for USAID and had a solid business mind, I might as well put it to good use.

I'd become good friends with USAID's IT manager, who was a computer wizard. And when I told him about my plan, we decided to collaborate. I put up the money, he offered the technological skills, and we hired a few additional engineers, including females, to better serve Arab women.

We named the company Electric Computer Systems, and I created some marketing materials. Our advertising included a man bringing a computer up some steps, with his son imploring him, "Papa, you don't have to do that" and asking him to phone our toll-free number.

Calls began to stream in, and we found ourselves unexpectedly prosperous. I purchased a new company van, we obtained a licence to sell HP equipment, and we expanded into networking. I was having the greatest time of my life. I didn't need the money at this point, but I was doing something productive and having fun.

* * *

Ever since I began my spiritual journey, I'd had some interesting discussions about Jesus and my evolving ideas with my Shin Bet buddies.

"Believe whatever you want," they instructed. "You are welcome to share it with us." But don't tell anyone else about it. And never, ever get baptised since that would be a very public declaration. If it was discovered that you converted a Christian and abandoned your Islamic beliefs, you could face serious consequences."

I don't think they were as concerned about my future as they were about their own. But God was changing my life too drastically for me to resist.

Jamal, one of my friends, was cooking dinner for me one day. "Mosab," he went on to say, "I have a surprise for you."

With a twinkle in his eye, he turned the channel and added, "Check out this TV program on Al-Hayat." It might be of interest to you."

I found myself looking into the eyes of Zakaria Botros, an elderly Coptic priest. He had a lovely appearance and a warm, engaging voice. I was fond of him until I discovered what he was saying. He was performing an autopsy on the Qur'an, opening it up and exposing every bone, muscle, sinew, and organ, then putting them under the microscope of truth and revealing that the entire book was diseased.

Inaccuracies in fact and history, contradictions—he exposed them exactly and respectfully, but firmly and with conviction. My immediate reaction was to lash out and turn off the television. But that only lasted a few seconds before I realised it was God's answer to my prayers. Father Zakaria was removing all the dead pieces of Allah that were still connecting me to Islam and blinding me to the fact that Jesus is the Son of God. I couldn't move further in following him until that happened. However, it was not an easy move. Consider the agony of discovering one day that your father is not truly your father.

I can't tell you when I "became a Christian" because it was a six-year journey. But I knew I was, and no matter what the Shin Bet said, I needed to get baptised. Around the same time, a group of American Christians travelled to Israel to explore the Holy Land and visit their sister church, which I was attending.

I became good friends with one of the girls in the group over time. I enjoyed talking with her and immediately trusted her. When I told her about my spiritual journey, she was quite encouraging, telling me that God often employs the most unexpected people to perform his work. That was certainly the case in my case.

My friend asked me why I hadn't gotten baptised one evening when we were having dinner at the American Colony Restaurant in East Jerusalem. I couldn't tell her it was because I was a Shin Bet operative, deeply involved in every political and security operation in the region. But it was a legitimate question, one I had asked myself numerous times.

"Can you baptise me?" I inquired. She stated that she could.

"Can you keep it a secret between us?"

She agreed, adding, "The beach isn't too far away." Let's get going."

"Are you serious?" "Sure, why not?" "Okay, why not?"

I was delighted when we took the shuttle to Tel Aviv. Is it possible that I had forgotten who I was? Was I truly putting my faith in this San Diego girl? We were wandering along the packed beach 45 minutes later, taking in the wonderful, balmy evening air. No one in the throng could have known that the son of Hamas's commander, who was responsible for the massacre of twenty-one children at the Dolphinarium just up the road, was about to be baptised as a Christian.

We stepped into the sea after I removed my shirt.

* * *

My father received a phone call as I was driving him back from one of the refugee camps near Ramallah on Friday, September 23, 2005.

"What is going on?" I could hear him barking into the phone. "What?" My father sounded irritated.

When he got off the phone, he told me that it was Hamas spokesman Sami Abu Zuhri in Gaza who had informed him that Israelis had just killed a huge number of Hamas members during a rally in the Jabaliya refugee camp. The caller insisted he saw Israeli planes drop missiles into the crowd. He said that they had broken the truce.

Just seven months ago, my father had worked very hard to broker that truce. It appeared like all of his efforts had been in vain. He'd never trusted Israel in the first place, and he was enraged by their desire for blood.

But I didn't buy it. Even though I didn't say anything to my father, something about the story didn't smell right.

Al-Jazeera contacted me. As soon as we arrived in Ramallah, they wanted my father on the air. We were at their studios in twenty minutes.

I called Loai while they were fitting my father with a microphone.

He informed me that no strike had been launched by Israel. I was furious. I requested that the producer show me the news footage of the incident. He led me to the control room, where we watched it over and over again. The explosion had clearly come from the ground up, rather than from the sky.

Sheikh Hassan Yousef was already on the air, shouting about Israel's treachery, threatening to break the truce, and demanding an international probe.

"So do you feel better now?" As he walked away from the set, I asked him. "What do you mean?"

"I mean after your statement."

"Why should I not feel better?" I still can't believe they did it."

"That's good, since they didn't. Hamas did it. Zuhri is a deceiver. I'd like to show you something, so please come to the control room." My father accompanied me back to the small room, where we watched the film several times more.

"Take a look at the explosion. Look. The blast moves from the bottom to the top. It didn't appear out of nowhere."

We later learned that the Hamas military guys in Gaza had been flaunting their equipment during the demonstration when a Qassam missile in the back of a pickup truck burst, killing fifteen people and injuring many more.

My father was taken aback. But Hamas was not alone in its deceptions and cover-ups. Despite what it could see in its own news video, Al-Jazeera kept broadcasting the lies. Then things got worse. Even terrible.

In retaliation for the false attack on Gaza, Hamas launched roughly forty missiles toward communities in southern Israel, the first major offensive since Israel's departure from Gaza a week before. My father and I, like the rest of the world, watched the news at home. The next day, Loai informed me that the cabinet had concluded that Hamas had violated the cease-fire.

According to a news report, Israel's army's chief of operations, Major General Israel Ziv, said: "It was decided to launch a prolonged and constant attack on Hamas," the correspondent stated, implying that Israel was ready to resume targeted attacks targeting key Hamas leaders, a practice that had been abandoned before the cease-fire.

"Your father has to go in," Loai explained. "Are you asking for my approval?"

"No. They're requesting him directly, and we can't help them."

I was enraged.

"However, my father did not fire any missiles last night." He did not request it. He had absolutely nothing to do with it. It was all because of those morons in Gaza."

I eventually ran out of energy. I was devastated. Loai broke the spell. "Are you there?"

"Yes." I took a seat. "This is not fair . . . but I understand." "You, too," he admitted gently.

"What, me, too?" Prison? Forget about it! I'm not returning. I'm not concerned with the cover. It's the end of the road for me. "I'm done."

"My brother," he said quietly, "do you think I want you arrested?" It is all up to you. If you want to go out, you go out. But this is a more hazardous period than any other. You've been by your father's side more than ever in the last year. Everyone knows you have a close relationship with Hamas. Many assume you are even a member of its leadership... You'll be dead in a few weeks if we don't arrest you."

Chapter 24: Good-Bye

"What's going on?" my father inquired when he discovered me sobbing.

When I didn't respond, he proposed we cook dinner for my mother and sisters together. My father and I had grown so close over the years, and he realised that there were times when I needed to work things out on my own.

My heart broke as I cooked lunch with him, knowing that these were the final hours we'd spend together for a long time. I decided not to leave him alone during his arrest.

I phoned Loai after dinner.

"All right," I said. "I will go back to prison."

The date was September 25, 2005. I hiked to a favourite area in the hills outside of Ramallah where I frequently went to pray and read my Bible. I prayed harder, grieved harder, and begged the Lord to have compassion on me and my family. I sat down and waited when I arrived home. My father had already gone to bed, blissfully unconscious of what was going to unfold. The security troops came just after midnight.

They led us to Ofer Prison, where we were crammed into a large hall with hundreds of other people apprehended in a citywide sweep. They also arrested my brothers Oways and Mohammad this time. Loai told me in private that they were suspects in a murder investigation. One of their classmates had kidnapped, tortured, and murdered an Israeli settler, and the Shin Bet had intercepted the killer's call to Oways the day before. Mohammad was set free a few days later. Oways would be imprisoned for four months before being absolved of any involvement in the crime.

For ten hours, we sat on our knees in that hall, our wrists tied behind us. When someone offered my father a chair and I saw that he was being handled with dignity, I silently thanked God.

I received a three-month administrative detention sentence. My Christian friends sent me a Bible, and I served my time while reading the Bible and going through the motions. On Christmas Day 2005, I was released. My father, on the other hand, was not. He is still in prison as I write this.

* * *

Parliamentary elections were approaching, and every Hamas leader wanted to run. They continued to disgust me. They were all free, while the single man fit to lead his people was imprisoned behind razor wire. After everything that had happened leading up to our incarceration, it didn't take much to persuade my father not to vote. He contacted me and asked that I inform Mohammad Daraghmeh, a political analyst with the Associated Press and a good friend, of his choice.

A few hours later, the news broke, and my phone began to ring. Hamas leaders attempted to contact my father in prison, but he refused to speak with them.

"What's going on?" they inquired. "What a disaster! We will lose because if your father does not run, it will appear that he has disapproved of the entire election!"

"If he doesn't want to participate," I went on to say, "you have to respect that."

Then followed a phone call from Ismail Haniyeh, the Hamas ticket's leader who would soon become the new PA prime minister.

"As a movement leader, I am asking you to call a press conference and announce that your father is still running for Hamas." Tell them the AP report was a mistake." On top of that, they asked me to lie for them. Were they unaware that Islam forbids lying, or did they believe it was acceptable because politics has no religion?

"I can't do that," I said. "I respect you, but I respect my father and my own integrity more." And then I hung up.

I received a death threat thirty minutes later. "Call the news conference immediately," said the caller, "or we will kill you."

"Come and kill me then."

I hung up and dialled Loai's number. The man who made the threat was apprehended within hours.

Death threats didn't bother me at all. When my father heard out, he personally called Daraghmeh and informed him he would vote in the election. He then advised me to relax and wait for his release. He told me that he would deal with Hamas.

Naturally, my father couldn't campaign from behind bars. He didn't have to, though. Hamas plastered his image everywhere, subtly pushing everyone to vote for the organisation's ticket. And on the eve of the election, Sheikh Hassan Yousef was carried into parliament, dragging everyone else along like a lion's mane.

* * *

I sold my stake in Electric Computer Systems to my partner because I felt that a lot of things in my life were coming to an end.

What exactly was I? What type of future might I see if things continued in this manner?

I was 27 years old, and I couldn't even date. My notoriety as the son of a major Hamas commander would frighten a Christian girl. A Muslim girl would not be interested in an Arab Christian. And what

Jewish girl would want to date Hassan Yousef's son? What would we talk about if someone went out with me? What was I allowed to say about my life? And what kind of life was it in the first place? What had I given up everything for? What about Palestine? What about Israel? For the sake of peace?

What did I get for being the Shin Bet's superspy? Were my ancestors better off? Was the bloodshed over? Was my father with his family at home? Was Israel more secure? Had I set a better example for my brothers and sisters? I felt like I'd wasted about a third of my life "chasing after the wind," as King Solomon describes it in Ecclesiastes 4:16.

I couldn't even tell you everything I'd learnt while wearing my various caps and hoods. Who'd trust me?

I dialled Loai's number from his office. "I cannot work for you anymore." "Why? "What occurred?"

"Nothing. I adore each and every one of you. And I enjoy working in intelligence. I believe I am addicted to my job. But we're not getting anywhere. We are engaged in a battle that cannot be won with arrests, interrogations, and assassinations. Our adversaries are ideas, and ideas are unconcerned about intrusions and curfews. With a Merkava, we can't blow out a concept. We don't have a problem with you, and we don't have a problem with you. We're all imprisoned in a maze, like rats. It's too much for me. "My time has come to an end."

I anticipated this would be a crushing blow to the Shin Bet. We were in the midst of a conflict.

"Okay," she replied, "I will inform the agency leadership and see what they say."

When we met again, he added, "Here is the leadership's offer. Israel has a large communications company." We will provide you with all of the funds you require to establish a similar organisation in the Palestinian territories. It's a fantastic chance that will ensure your future for the rest of your life."

"You don't get it. My issue is not one of money. My issue is that I'm not going anywhere."

"People here need you, Mosab."

"I'll find a different way to help them, but not in this way." Even the agency is unsure where it is going."

"So what do you want?"

"I want to leave the country."

He told his bosses about our talk. We went back and forth, the leadership insisting that I stay while I stressed that I had to leave.

"Okay," they said. "We'll let you go to Europe for several months, maybe a year, as long as you promise to come back."

"I'm not going to Europe." I wish to visit the United States. I have acquaintances there. Perhaps I'll return in a year, two years, or five years. I have no idea. Right now, all I know is that I need a break."

"The United States will be difficult. You have money, power, and are safe from everyone. You've established a strong reputation, founded a nice business, and lived comfortably. Do you know what your life would be like in the United States? You will be insignificant and have no impact."

I told them I didn't mind if I had to do the dishes. When I persisted, they planted their feet.

"No," they said. "There is no United States. Only Europe, and only for a limited period. Have fun. We'll continue to pay your wage. Simply go have fun. Take a breather. Then come back."

"Okay," I finally said, "I'm going home." I'm not doing anything for you anymore. I'm not going to leave the house because I don't want to come across a suicide bomber and have to report it. Don't bother calling me. "I no longer work for you."

I went to my folks' house and turned off my cell phone. My beard got long and thick. My mother was always checking on me and asking if I was okay. Day after day, I read my Bible, listened to music, watched television, reflected on the previous 10 years, and struggled with depression.

After three months, my mother called and asked for me. I told her I didn't want to talk to anyone. However, she stated that the caller stated that it was urgent, that he was an old acquaintance, and that he knew my father.

I went downstairs and took up the receiver. It was a Shin Bet agent.

"We want to see you," the caller said. "It's critical. We have fantastic news for you."

I went to the meeting. My inability to work had put them in a bind. They could tell I was determined to quit.

"Okay, we'll let you go to the United States, but only for a few months, and you have to promise to come back."

"I don't know why you keep insisting on something you know you're not going to get," I said quietly but firmly.

Finally, they said, "All right, we'll let you go with two conditions." First, you must employ a lawyer and petition the court to allow you to leave the nation for medical reasons. Otherwise, you will get burned. Second, you've returned."

The Shin Bet never allowed Hamas members to cross the border unless they needed medical treatment that was not available in the

Palestinian territory. I had a jaw condition that prevented me from closing my teeth together, and I couldn't undergo the treatment I needed in the West Bank. It had never troubled me much, but I decided it was as good an excuse as any, so I hired a lawyer to write a medical report to the court, requesting permission for me to fly to the United States for the operation.

The entire point of this effort was to produce a clear paper trail before the courts and demonstrate that I was battling a hostile bureaucracy in an attempt to escape Israel. If the Shin Bet let me go without a fight, it would imply favouritism, and people may start to ask what I had offered them in exchange. So we had to make it appear as if they were making it difficult for me and battling me every step of the way.

However, the lawyer I chose proved to be a hindrance. He apparently didn't think I stood a chance, so he demanded his money in advance, which I gave, and then sat back and did nothing. The Shin Bet had no papers to create because they had received nothing from my counsel. I called him every week to see how my case was going. The only thing he had to do was complete the papers, but he continued procrastinating and lying. He said that there was an issue. There were difficulties. He kept saying he needed more money, and I kept paying him.

This carried on for six months. Finally, on New Year's Day 2007, I received a phone call.

"You're approved to leave," the lawyer stated, as if he had just solved the world's hunger problem.

* * *

"Can you meet just one more time with one of the Hamas leaders in the Jalazone refugee camp?" Loai enquired. "You're the only person—"

"I'm leaving the country in five hours."

"OK," he murmured, surrendering. "Be safe and stay in touch with us." Call once you pass the border to ensure that everything is in order."

I called some people I knew in California and informed them I was coming. Of course, they had no idea I was the son of a key Hamas leader and a Shin Bet agent. But they were ecstatic. I grabbed a few clothes in a small suitcase and went downstairs to tell my mother. She was already in bed.

I knelt at her side and told that I would be departing in a few hours, crossing the border into Jordan and travelling to the United States. Even then, I couldn't explain why.

Her eyes told it all. Your father is imprisoned. You are like a father figure to your brothers and sisters. What will you do in America? I knew she didn't want me to leave, but she also wanted me to be happy. She expressed her optimism that I would be able to establish a life for myself there after being in such danger at home. She had no idea how much danger I had seen.

"Please allow me to kiss you goodbye," she pleaded. "Wake me in the morning before you go."

She blessed me, and I informed her I was leaving very early and she didn't need to get up to see me off. But she was my mother. She stayed up all night with me in our living room, together with my brothers and sisters and my friend Jamal.

I was going to pack my Bible—the one with all my notes, the one I had studied for years, even in prison—when I felt an urging to give it to Jamal.

"I don't have a more expensive gift to give you before I leave," I said to him. "This is my Bible." Read it and follow it." I was confident that he would respect my desires and would read it anytime he thought of me. I made sure I had enough money, left the house, and went to the Allenby Bridge, which connects Israel and Jordan.

It was easy to pass via the Israeli checkpoint. I paid the $35 exit tax and entered the massive immigration terminal with its metal detectors, X-ray scanners, and the infamous Room 13 where suspects were interrogated. However, these devices, along with strip searches, were largely for people entering Israel from Jordan, not those leaving.

The terminal was a hive of people wearing shorts and fanny packs, yarmulkes and Arab headdresses, veils and ball caps, some wearing backpacks and others pushing hand trolleys packed with bags. Finally, I boarded one of the large JETT buses—the only public conveyance permitted across the concrete truss bridge.

Okay, I thought, it's almost done.

But I was still a little paranoid. The Shin Bet simply did not allow people like me to leave the country. It was unheard of. Even Loai was surprised that I had obtained permission.

When I arrived in Jordan, I handed in my passport. I was worried because, while my US visa was valid for three years, my passport was set to expire in less than thirty days.

Please, I begged, just let me enter Jordan for one day. That's all I need. But all of my anxiety was for naught. There was no issue. I took a taxi into Amman and booked a flight with Air France. I settled into a hotel for a few hours before heading to Queen Alia International Airport to board my aircraft to California via Paris.

As I sat on the plane, I reflected on all I had just left behind, both good and bad—my family and friends, as well as the endless bloodshed, waste, and futility.

It took some time to get used to the idea of being truly free—free to be myself, free of covert meetings and Israeli prisons, free of always looking over my shoulder.

It was odd. And wonderful.

* * *

One day while walking down the street in California, I noticed a familiar face approaching me. It was the face of Maher Odeh, the mastermind behind so many suicide bombings—the same guy I had witnessed being visited by Arafat's armed goons in 2000. I eventually identified them as the foundation cell of the eerie Al-Aqsa Martyrs Brigades.

At first, I wasn't entirely certain it was Odeh. People appear differently when they are not in their natural environment. I hoped I was mistaken. Hamas has never attempted a martyrdom operation in the United States. It would be horrible for the United States if he was here. It would be harmful to me as well.

Our gazes locked for a split second. I swear I saw a flash of recognition there before he continued down the street.

Printed in Great Britain
by Amazon